JACK JO

MW00377677

This book was approved by Jack Johnson

This book was printed on recycled paper, using soy based ink.
To learn more about Jack Johnson's green efforts, please visit JackJohnsonMusic.com/greening, and AllAtOnce.org.

Cherry Lane Music Company
Director of Publications/Project Editor: Mark Phillips

ISBN: 978-1-60378-379-8

Visit our website at www.cherrylaneprint.com

CONTENTS

4 ANGEL

6 BANANA PANCAKES

12 BETTER TOGETHER

9 BREAKDOWN

16 BUBBLE TOES

20 COCOON

23 COOKIE JAR

26 CRYING SHAME

30 CUPID

34 DO YOU REMEMBER

36 DREAMS BE DREAMS

31 DRINK THE WATER

38 F-STOP BLUES

40 FALL LINE

42 FLAKE

48 FORTUNATE FOOL

45 FROM THE CLOUDS

50 GONE

52 GOOD PEOPLE

56 HOLES TO HEAVEN

58 THE HORIZON HAS BEEN DEFEATED

64 IF I COULD

61 IF I HAD EYES

66 INAUDIBLE MELODIES

69 LOSING HOPE

72 MIDDLE MAN

75 MUDFOOTBALL (FOR MOE LERNER)

78 NEVER KNOW

84 NO OTHER WAY

86 POSTERS

89 RODEO CLOWNS

92 SEXY PLEXI

94 SITTING, WAITING, WISHING

100 STAPLE IT TOGETHER

97 TAYLOR

102 TIMES LIKE THESE

105 TOMORROW MORNING

108 TRAFFIC IN THE SKY

111 UPSIDE DOWN

114 WASTING TIME

117 YOU AND YOUR HEART

Angel

Words and Music by
Jack Johnson

Eb	Gm	Cm	Ab	Fm7	Bb
3 4 1	2 3 1	3 3 3	3 1 2 1	1 3 1 4	3 2 1 1

Intro

Eb　　　|Gm　　　|Cm　　　|Ab　　　|

Fm7　　　|Bb　　　|Eb　　　|

Verse 1

　　　‖Eb　　　|Gm

I've got an an - gel;

　　　　　　|Cm　　　|Ab

She doesn't wear any wings.

　　　|Fm7

She wears a heart　　that can melt my own;

　　　|Bb　　　　　　　　|Eb　　　|

She wears a smile　　that can make me wanna sing.

Verse 2

　　　‖Eb　　　|Gm

She gives me presents

　　　　　|Cm　　　|Ab

With her presence alone.

　　|Fm7

She gives me ev - 'rything I could wish for;

　　|Bb　　　　　　|Eb　　　|

She gives me kiss - es on the lips just for coming　home.

Verse 3

   ‖Eb |Gm
She can make angels;

     |Cm |Ab
Seen it with my own eyes.

     |Fm7
You gotta be care - ful when you've got good love,

    |Bb |Eb |
'Cause them an - gels will just keep on multiply - ing.

Outro

   ‖Fm7 |Bb
But you're so busy changing the world.

    |Fm7 |Bb
Just one smile and you could change all of mine.

      |Eb Gm |Cm
We share the same soul. Oh, oh, oh, oh.

     |Eb Gm |Cm
Share the same soul. Oh, oh, oh, oh.

     |Eb Gm |Cm
Share the same soul. Oh, oh, oh, oh.

    |Ab Fm7 |Eb   ‖
Oh, oh, oh, oh. Mm, mm, mm, mm.

Banana Pancakes

Words and Music by Jack Johnson

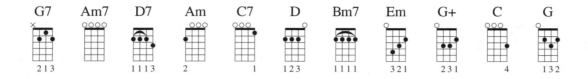

Intro

G7 |Am7

Well, can't you see that it's just raining?

Am7 |G7

There ain't no need to go out - side.

Verse 1

D7·   ‖G7   D7

But baby, you hardly even notice

Am   C7 |G7

When I try to show you this song,

D7 |Am   C7

It's meant to keep you from doing what you're s'posed to.

G7   D7

Waking up too early,

Am   C7

Maybe we could sleep in.

G7   D7

Make you banana pancakes,

|Am   C7 |Am

Pre - tend like it's the weekend now.

Am |G7

And we could pretend it all the time,   yeah.

G7 |Am

Can't you see that it's just raining?

Am |G7

There ain't no need to go out - side.

Verse 2

```
G7           D7        ‖G7          D7               |
    But just maybe ha - la ka uku - lele,
```

```
Am           C7
Mama made a baby.
```

```
 |G7                    D7
(I) really don't mind the practice,
```

```
      |Am           C7                |
'Cause you're my little lady.
```

```
G7           D7
Lady, lady, love me,
```

```
      |Am               C7           |
'Cause I love to lay here, lazy.
```

```
G7                   D7
We could close the curtains,
```

```
      |Am               C7       ·|Am              |
Pre - tend like there's no world out  -   side.
```

```
Am                                |G7           |
    And we could pretend it all the time,  no.
```

```
G7                            |Am          |
    Can't you see that it's just raining?
```

```
Am                              |G7          |
    There ain't no need to go out - side.
```

```
G7                       |Am           |
    Ain't no need, ain't no need.
```

```
Am                        |G7           |
    Mm, mm, mm, mm.
```

```
G7                          |Am          |
    Can't you see, can't you see?
```

```
Am                              |G7          |
    Rain all day and I don't mind.
```

Bridge

‖Am7 |
But the telephone is singing, ringing;

Am7 |D |
It's just too early, don't pick it up.

D
　We don't need to;

　　　|Am7
We got ev'rything we need right here,

　　|Am7 |D |
And everything we need is enough.

D |Bm7 |
　(It's) just so easy when the whole world fits in - side of your arms.

　　|Em   G+ |C
Do we really need to pay attention to the alarm?

　　　|G |D7 |G |
Wake up slow.   Mm, mm.   Wake up slow.

Repeat Verse 1

Outro

G7 |Am7 |
　Ain't no need, ain't no need.

Am7 |G7 |
　Rain all day and I real - ly, really, really don't mind.

G7 |Am7 |
　Can't you see, can't you see?

Am7 |G   ‖
　We've got to wake up slow.

Breakdown

Words and Music by
Jack Johnson, Dan Nakamura and Paul Huston

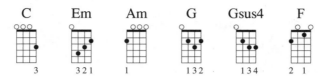

Verse 1

C |Em
I hope this old train breaks down.

Am |G
Then I could take a walk around and

C |Em
See what there is to see.

Am |G
Time is just a melody.

        |C
With all the people in the street

    |Em
Walking fast as their feet can take them,

Am |G
I   just roll through town.

       |C
And though my window's got a view,

     |Em
Well, the frame I'm looking through

    |Am |G ||
Seems to have no concern for me now.   So for now I...

Chorus

```
         C     |Gsus4         |Am            |G              |
             I   need  this here      old train  to break down.

         C     |Gsus4         |Am                |G           ||
             Oh, please  just        let me please  break down.
```

Interlude

```
         C        |Em        |Am        |G            |
         C        |Em        |Am        |G            ||
```

Verse 2

```
         C                      |Em                    |
             Well, this engine  screams  out loud;

      Am                     |G                 |
          Centipede   gonna  crawl  westbound.

      C                     |Em                   |
          So I don't even  make  a sound, 'cause

      Am                            |G
          It's gonna  sting me  when I  leave this town.

               |C                        |Em
      And all  the people  in the  street  that I'll never  get to  meet

           |Am                            |
      (If) these    tracks don't  bend  somehow.

      G    |C                   |Em
           And I got no time  that I    got to  get to

         |Am                       |G            ||
      Where    I don't  need to be.        So I...
```

Repeat Chorus (2x)

Bridge

```
        C    |G        F              |C    |G      F          |
                 I wanna break on down.        But I can't stop now.
        C    |G        F          |C       |G      F
                 Let me break on down.
```

Verse 3

```
                  ||C                    |Em
        But you can't stop nothing if you got no control
            |Am                          |G
        Of the thoughts in your mind that you kept in, you know.
            |C                       |Em
        You don't know nothing, but you don't need to know.
            |Am                      |G
        The wisdom's in the trees, not the glass windows.
            |C                    |Em
        You can't stop wishing if you don't let go,
            |Am                      |G
        The things that you find and you lose and you know.
            |C                    |Em
        You keep on rolling, put the moment on hold.
            |Am                         |G                    ||
        The frame's too bright so put the blinds down low. And...
```

Repeat Chorus (2x)

Outro

```
        C     |Em      |Am      |G


                            |C      |Em      |Am      |G
        I wanna break on down.
                            |C      |Em      |Am      |G      ·  |
        But I can't stop now.
        C     |Em      |Am      |G      |C       ||
```

Better Together

Words and Music by Jack Johnson

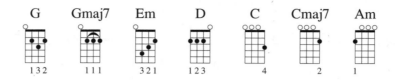

Verse 1

   G   **Gmaj7**
There's no combi - nation of words

      |**Em**   **D**
I could put on the back of a postcard,

C   **Cmaj7**
No song that I   could sing.

    |**Am**   **D** |
But I could try for your heart and

G **Gmaj7** |**Em**   **D**
Our dreams, and they are made out of real things,

    |**C**   **Cmaj7**
Like a   shoebox of photographs

   |**Am**   **D** |
With sepiatone loving.

G   **Gmaj7**
Love is the answer,

     |**Em**   **D**
At least for most of the questions in my heart,

  |**C**   **Cmaj7** |**Am**
Like, "Why are we here?" and "Where do we go?"

         D
And "How come it's so hard?"

 |**G**   **Gmaj7**
And it's not always easy,

   |**Em**   **D** |
And sometimes life can be de - ceiving.

C   **Cmaj7**
I'll tell you one thing,

 |**Am**   **D** ||
It's always better when we're to - gether.

Chorus

```
        C              |D                            |
        Mm, it's always better when we're together.
        C                    |D                           |
        Yeah, we'll look at the stars when we're together.
        C              |D                            |
        Well, it's always better when we're together.
        C                |D                             ||
        Yeah, it's always better when we're together.
```

Interlude

```
        G    Gmaj7   |Em   D   |C   Cmaj7    |Am   D    |

        G    Gmaj7   |Em   D   |C   Cmaj7    |Am   D
```

Verse 2

     ‖**G**
And all of these moments

     Gmaj7 |**Em**   **D** |
Just might find their way into my dreams tonight,

    |**C**   **Cmaj7**
But I know that they'll be gone

     |**Am**   **D**
When the morning light sings

     |**G**   **Gmaj7**
Or brings new things.

    |**Em**   **D**
For to - morrow night you see

   |**C**   **Cmaj7**
That they'll be gone too.

    |**Am**   **D**
Too many things I have to do.

      |**G**   **Gmaj7**
But if all of these dreams might find their way

    |**Em**   **D**
Into my day - to - day scene,

    |**C**   **Cmaj7**
I'd be under the impres - sion

    |**Am**   **D** |**G**
I was somewhere in between with only two,

      Gmaj7
Just me and you.

     |**Em**   **D**
Not so many things we got to do

   |**C**   **Cmaj7**
Or places we got to be.

     |**Am**   **D**   ‖
We'll sit be - neath the mango tree now.

Chorus

C |D
Yeah, it's always better when we're together.

C |D
Mm, we're somewhere in between together.

C |D
Well, it's always better when we're together.

C |D
Yeah, it's always better when we're together.

Interlude

G   Gmaj7 |Em   D |C   Cmaj7 |Am   D |

G   Gmaj7 |Em   D |C   Cmaj7 |Am   D ||

Bridge

Am |D
I believe in memo - ries;

|Am |D
They look so,   so pretty when I sleep.

|Am |D
Hey now, and,   and when I wake   up,

|Am
You look so pretty

|D
Sleeping next to me.

|C |D
But there is   not enough time,

|C |D
And there is no,   no song I could sing.

|C |D
And there is no   combination of words I could say,

|C |
But I will still   tell you one thing:

D ||
We're better together.

Outro

G   Gmaj7 |Em   D |C   Cmaj7 |Am   D |

G   Gmaj7 |Em   D |C   Cmaj7 |Am   D |G ||

Bubble Toes

Words and Music by Jack Johnson

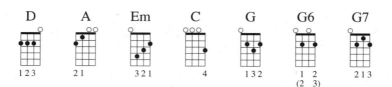

Intro

    |D   A

It's as simple as something that nobody knows,

    |Em   C

That her eyes are as big as her bubbly toes,

    |D   A

On the feet of a queen of the hearts of the cards,

    |E   C |G G6 |G7   G6

And her feet are all covered with tar balls and scars.

    |D   A

It's as common as something that nobody knows,

    |Em   C

That her beauty will follow wher - ever she goes,

    |D   A

Up the hill in the back of her house in the…

         |Em

Would she love me forever?

C |G   G6 |G7   G6

I know she could.

       |D   A |

I re - member when you and me,

Em   C |D

Mm, how we used to be just good friends.

        A |

Wouldn't give me none,

Em   C |G |C D G |C D ||

But all I wanted was some.

Verse 1

```
        G
She's got a whole lotta reasons,
                      |C                D
She can't think of a single one that can justify leaving.
    |G                                              |C
And he got none, but he thinks he got so many prob - lems,
          |D                    |G        |C   D
Man, he got too much time to waste.
    |G
His dreams are like commercials,
      |C                  D
But her dreams are picture per - fect,
      |G
And our dreams are so related,
            |C        D      |G       |C   D
Though they're often under - estimated.
```

Chorus

```
      ‖G
It's as simple as something that nobody knows,
      |C                    D
That her eyes are as big as her bub - bly toes,
        |G
On the feet of a queen of the hearts of the cards,
        |C                  D            |
(And her) feet are infested with tar   balls and . . .
G                            |
La, da, da, da, da, da.
C            D               |
  La, da, da, da,  da, da, da.
G                            |
La, da, da, da, da, da.
C              D          |G     |C  D |G      |C   D
  La, da, da, da,  da, da, da, da.
```

Verse 2

‖**G**
Well, I was eating lunch at the D.L.G.

|**C**   **D** |
When this little girl came and she sat next to me.

G
Never seen nobody move the way she did.

|**C** **N.C.**
Well, she did and she does and she'll do it again.

|**G**
When you move like a jellyfish, rhythm don't mean nothing.

|**C**   **D** |
You go with the flow, you don't stop.

G   **N.C.**
Move like a jellyfish, rhythm is nothing.

|**C**   **D** |**G** |**C** **D**
You go with the flow, you don't stop. Mm.

‖**G**

Chorus
It's as common as something that nobody knows,

|**C**   **D**
That her beau - ty will follow wherev - er she goes,

|**G**
Up the hill in the back of her house in the wood.

|**C**   **D** |
She'll love me forever, I know   she …

G |
La, da, da, da, da, da.

C   **D** |
  La, da, da, da, da, da, da.

G |
La, da, da, da, da, da.

C   **D** |**G** |
  La, da, da, da, da, da, da, da.

Bridge

‖**G**
If you would only listen,

|**C**   **D**
You might just realize what you're miss - ing,

|**G** |**C**   **D**
You're missing me.

|**G**
If you would only listen,

|**C**   **D**
You might just realize what you're miss - ing,

|**G** |**C**   **D**
You're missing me.

Chorus

‖**G**
It's as simple as something that nobody knows,

|**C**   **D**
That her eyes   are as big as her bub - bly toes,

|**G**
On the feet of a queen of the hearts of the cards,

|**C**   **D** |
(And her) feet are infested with tar   balls and . . .

G |
La, da, da, da, da, da.

C   **D** |
  La, da, da, da,   da, da, da.

G |
La, da, da, da, da, da.

C   **D** |
  La, da, da, da,   da, da, da.

G |
La, da, da, da, da, da.

C   **D** |
  La, da, da, da,   da, da, da.

G |
La, da, da, da, da, da.

C   **D** |**G** | ‖
  La, da, da, da,   da, da, da, da.

Cocoon

Words and Music by Jack Johnson

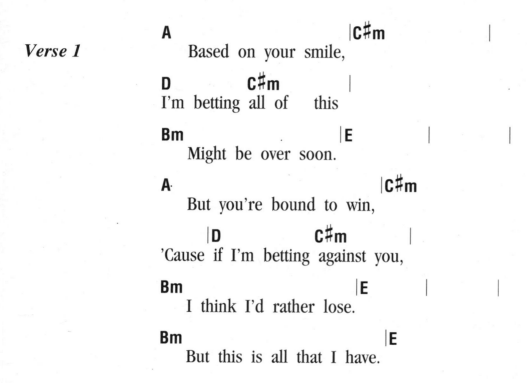

Verse 1

A |C#m |
Based on your smile,

D   C#m |
I'm betting all of   this

Bm |E | |
Might be over soon.

A |C#m
But you're bound to win,

|D   C#m |
'Cause if I'm betting against you,

Bm |E | |
I think I'd rather lose.

Bm |E
But this is all that I have.

Chorus

‖A   G# |
So please,

D   E |A   G# |
Take what's left of this heart and   use,

D   E |A   G# |
Please use only what you really   need.

D   E |A   G# |
You know I only have so little, so   please,

D   E |A   E |A   E   ‖
Mend your broken heart and   leave.

Verse 2

```
        A                          |C♯m
           I know it's not your style

              |D        C♯m              |
        And I can  tell by the way that you move

        Bm                     |E        |          |
           It's real, real soon.

        A                          |C♯m
           But I'm on your side

              |D        C♯m              |
        And I don't want to be your regret.

        Bm                          |E      |          |
           I'd rather be your cocoon.

        Bm                              |E
           But this is all that you have.
```

Chorus

```
        ‖A       G♯        |
        So    please,

        D                      E                      |A       G♯        |
           Let me take what's left of your heart and I will   use,

        D          E          |A       G♯     |
           I swear I'll use only what I   need.

        D                  E
           I know you only have so little,

           |A       G♯        |
        So    please,

        D                      E                      ‖
           Let me mend my broken heart and....
```

Bridge

    A   **|C♯m**   **|**
    You said this was all you have   and it's all I need,

F♯m   **|D**   **|**
   But blah, blah, blah,   because it fell apart and

A   **|c♯m**   **|**
   I guess it's all you knew,   and all I had.

F♯m   **|D**
   But now we have   only confused hearts,

     |Bm   **|E**
And   I guess all we have   is really all we need.

Chorus

     ||A   **G♯**   **|**
So   please,

D   **E**   **|A**   **G♯**   **|**
Let's take these broken hearts and use,

D   **E**   **|A**   **G♯**   **|**
Let's use only what we really need.

D   **E**
You know we only have so little,

   |A   **G♯**   **|**
So,   please,

D   **E**   **|A**   **E**   **|A**   **E**   **|A**   **||**
Take these broken hearts and leave.

Cookie Jar

Words and Music by Jack Johnson

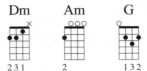

Verse 1

Dm Am |
I would turn on the TV,

G   Am |
But it's so embarrassing

Dm   Am |
To see all the other people.

G   Am ||
I don't know that they mean.

Verse 2

Dm   Am |
And it was magic at first,

G   Am |
When they spoke without sound.

Dm   Am |
But now this world is gonna hurt.

G   Am |
You better turn that thing down.

Dm Am |G Am ||
  Turn it around.

Verse 3

    Dm   Am
"It wasn't me," says   the boy with the gun.

           |G   Am
"Sure, I pulled the trigger but it needed to be done,

           |Dm   Am
Because life's   been killing me ev - er since it begun.

    |G   Am |Dm Am |G   Am
You can't blame me 'cause I'm too young."

Verse 4

    ‖Dm   Am
"You can't blame me. Sure,   the killer was my son,

    |G   Am
But I didn't teach him to pull the trigger of the gun.

    |Dm   Am
It's the   killing on his TV screen.

   |G   Am |Dm Am |G   Am
You can't blame me; it's those images he seen."

Verse 5

    ‖Dm   Am |
"Well, you can't blame me," says   the media man.

G   Am |
"I wasn't the one who came up with the plan.

Dm   Am
I   just point my camera at what the people want to see.

    |G   Am |Dm Am |G   Am
Man, it's a two-way mirror and you can't blame me."

Verse 6

    ‖Dm   Am
"You can't blame me," says   the singer of the song

    |G   Am
Or the maker of the movie which he based his life on.

    |Dm   Am
"It's only entertainment,   as anyone can see.

   |G   Am |Dm Am |G   Am
It's smoke machines and makeup. Man, you can't fool me."

Verse 7

```
       ‖Dm              Am
It was you; it was me; it   was every man.

          |G        Am
We've all   got the blood on our hands.

       |Dm            Am
We only receive what we demand,

       |G              Am                    |Dm  Am    |G    Am    ‖
And if we want hell, then hell's what we'll have.
```

Verse 8

```
Dm    Am                       |
   I   would turn on the TV,

G     Am                       |
   But it's so embarrassing

Dm    Am                          |
   To see all the other people

G        Am                         ‖
   Don't even know what they mean.
```

Verse 9

```
Dm     Am                     |
   And it   was magic at first,

G     Am                      |
   But    let everyone down.

Dm    Am                           |
   And now this world is gonna hurt.

G        Am                     |
   You better turn it around.

Dm    Am    |G    Am              |Dm          ‖
                     Turn it around.
```

Crying Shame

Lyrics by Jack Johnson
Music by Jack Johnson and Adam Topol

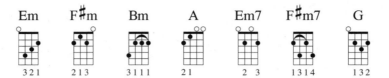

Intro

Em |F♯m |Em
            It's such a tired game.

     |F♯m
Will it ever stop?

         |Em
How will this all play out of sight,

    |F♯m   ‖
Out of mind, now?

Verse 1

F♯m |
By now we should know how to com - municate

|Bm
Instead of coming to blows. We're on a roll,

A |Bm
And there ain't no stopping us now.

A |Bm
We're burning under con - trol.

A |Bm A |F♯m
Isn't it strange how we're all burning under the same sun?

|
Buy now and save; it's a war for peace.

F♯m
It's the same old game,

|Bm
But do we really want to play?

A |Bm
We could close our eyes; it's still there.

A |Bm
We could say it's us against them.

A |
We could try but nobody wins.

Bm A ‖Em7
Grav - ity has got a hold on us all.

Pre-Chorus

       |F♯m7 |Em7
Could try to put it out, but it's a growing flame.

      |F♯m7 |Em7
Using fear as fuel, burning down our name.

        |F♯m7 |Em7
And it won't take too long, 'cause words all burn the same.

        |F♯m7
And who we gonna blame   now? And oh,

Chorus

       ‖Bm   A |G   F♯m
It's such a cry - ing, cry - ing, cry - ing shame.

       |Bm   A |G   F♯m
It's such a cry - ing, cry - ing, cry - ing shame.

       |Bm   A |G   F♯m |Em | ‖
It's such a cry - ing, cry - ing, cry - ing shame, shame, shame.

Interlude Bm A |Bm A |Bm A |Bm A ‖

Verse 2

F♯m
By now it's beginning to show;

|F♯m |Bm
A number of people are numbers that ain't coming home.

A |Bm
I could close my eyes, it's still there;

A |
Close my mind, be alone.

Bm   A |Bm
  I could close my heart and not care,

          A |F♯m
But grav - ity has got a hold on us all.

                                     |
It's a terrific price to pay.

F♯m |
   But in the true sense of the word,

Bm   A |
  Are we using   what we've learned?

Bm   A |
  In the true sense of the word,

Bm   A |
  Are we losing what we were?

Bm   A   ‖Em7
  It's   such a tired game.

                       |F♯m7 |Em7
Pre-Chorus Will it ever stop? It's not for me to say.

                           |F♯m7 |Em7
And is it in our blood, or is it just our fate?

                           |F♯m7 |Em7
And how will this all play out of sight, out mind, now?

                           |F♯m7
Who we gonna blame,   all in all?

Repeat Chorus

Cupid

Words and Music by Jack Johnson

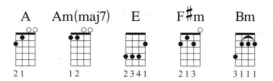

A   Am(maj7)   E   F♯m   Bm

Verse

|A   Am(maj7) |E   F♯m
Well, how man - y times must we go   through this?

|A   Am(maj7) |E   F♯m |
You always been mine, woman; I thought you   knew this.

A   Am(maj7) |E   F♯m
  How man - y times must we go   through this?

|A   Am(maj7) |E   F♯m |Bm |E
You always be mine; Cupid on - ly   misses some - times.

|A   Am(maj7) |E   F♯m |
Mm,   hmm.

|A   Am(maj7) |E   F♯m
Mm,   hmm.

Chorus

‖Bm |E
But we could end up brokenhearted

|A   Am(maj7) |F♯m
If   we don't remember   why   all this all started.

|Bm |E
And if   they try to tell you love fades with time,

|A   Am(maj7) |F♯m
Tell them   there's no such thing as time.

|Bm   E |A   Am(maj7) |
It's our   time.   It's our   time.

E   F♯m |A   Am(maj7) |E   F♯m |A   ‖
   It's our   time.   It's our   time.

Drink the Water

Words and Music by Jack Johnson

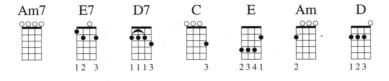

Verse 1

Am7
Drink the water, drink it down.

Am7
This time I know I'm bound

|**E7**
To spit it back up.

D7 |**Am7**
I didn't want this salty substitute;

Am7
Just not goin' to do.

|**E7**
I need some air

D7 |**Am7**
If I'm going to live through this experience.

Am7 |**E7**
Reminds me of a clock that just won't tick.

D7
I want to wake up

Am7
From this concussion,

Am7
But my dream is just not done.

|**E7**
I'm late again.

D7 |**Am7**
It's just one of those bad days.

                    |**Am7**
Look outside and   be careful what you ride.

|**E7** |**D7**
You just might find   that you're out of...

Chorus

```
        C              |E          |Am          |
        Time to swim       ashore.

        Am         |C                    |
         If I drift     long enough,

        E                    |Am         |              ||
            I'll be home.
```

Verse 2

```
        Am7                          |
            He's got delusions between   his ears,

                     |E7                    |D7       |
        Man, it takes    up too much space.

        Am7                         |
            And all that tension between   his gears,

                     |E7                    |D7
        Man, he'll nev - er ever leave this place.

             |Am7
        He's got stones instead of bones,

            |Am7                  |
        And everybody knows,

        E7                       |D7
           Ah, man, that can make you real, real slow.

            |Am7
        And if heaven was below,

                |Am7              |
        He'd know just where to go.

        E7
           Dive in the ocean,

                |D7                          ||
        And he'd sink like a stone, and he'd say,
```

Chorus

     C |**E** |**Am** |
"It's time to swim   ashore.

Am |**C** |
    If I drift   long enough,

E |**Am** | ‖
  I'll be home."

Bridge

Am
Hold on if you can;

           |**Am**
You're gonna sink faster

                  |**E** |**D**
Than you can imag - ine, so hold.

       |**Am**
Ah, just hold on if you can;

           |**Am**
You're gonna sink faster

                  |**E** |**D**
Than you can imag - ine, so hold.

Chorus

           ‖**C** |**E** |**Am** |
It's just time   to swim   ashore.

Am |**C** |
    If I drift   long enough,

E |**Am**   ‖
  I'll be home.

Do You Remember

Words and Music by Jack Johnson

C   G   F   Fmaj7   Dm   Em

Verse 1

‖**C**

Do you re - member   when   we first met?

G   **|F**   **|C**

I sure do.   It was some - time in   early Sep - tember.

G   **|C**   **|G**

Well, you were lazy about   it; you made me wait around.

|F   **|C**

I was so crazy about   you, I didn't mind.

G   **|C**   **|G**

So I was late for   class;   I locked my bike to yours.

|F   **|C**   **G**

It wasn't hard to find;   you painted flowers on it.

|C   **|G**

Guess that I was afraid   that if you rolled away

|F   **|C**   **G**

You might not roll back my direc - tion real soon.

Chorus

‖**G**

Well, I was crazy 'bout   you then

|G

And now, but the cra - ziest thing of all,

|Fmaj7   **|C**   **|Dm**

Over ten   years have gone   by

Dm

And you're still mine.   We're locked in time.

Dm   **|G**   **|F**   **|Em**

Let's re - wind.

Verse 2

```
Dm            ‖C              |                    |G         |
    Do you re - member when    we first moved in togeth - er?
              |F       |         |C              |
The pi - ano took up the living room.
G             |C              |                    |G            |
    You'd play me boogie - woog - ie; I'd play you love  songs.
                    |F              |                |C              |
You'd say we're playing     house;      now you still say we are.
G             |C      |              |G          |
    We built our getaway     up in a tree we found.
              |F      |              |C              |
We felt so far away,      but we were still in town.
G             |C              |                    |G            |
    Now, I re - member  watch - ing   that old tree burn  down.
              |F      |              |C          |G
I took a picture that     I don't like to look at.
```

Chorus

```
              ‖G              |
Well, all these times, they come and go,

              |G              |
And alone   don't seem so long.

              |Fmaj7    |C          |Dm          |
Over ten    years   have gone by.
Dm              |          |              |          |
    We can't re - wind.      We're locked in time.
Dm              |G      |F          |Em          |
    But you're still  mine.
Dm              |C          ‖
    Do you re - member?
```

Dreams Be Dreams

Words and Music by Jack Johnson

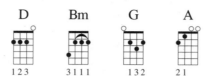

Verse 1

D   Bm |G   A |
She's just waiting for the sum - mertime, when the weath - er's fine.

D   Bm |G   A
She could hitch a ride   out of town and so far away

            |D   Bm |G   A
From that low - down,   good for noth - ing,

            |D   Bm |G
Mis - take - making fool with ex - cuses like,

Chorus

A ||D |Bm
"Baby, that was a long   time ago."

   |G |
But that's just a euphemism.

A
If you want the truth,

       |D |Bm
He was out   of control.

  |G |
But a short time's a long time

A ||
When your mind just won't let it go.

Verse 2

```
D                            Bm           |G                    A
 Well, summer came a - long and then it was gone and so was she;
   |D          Bm                     |G                    A
But   not from him,    'cause he followed her   just to let her know
   |D                 Bm              |
Her dreams are dreams
G        A         |D             Bm         |
 And all this living's so much harder than it seems.
G           A        |D     Bm         |
 But, girl, don't   let your dreams be dreams.
G             A       |D        Bm           |
 You know this living's not so hard as it seems.
G       A    |D  Bm  |G    A    |D   Bm    |G    A
 Don't let   your   dreams                be dreams,
   |D   Bm  |G   A   |D    Bm  |G   A   |D           ||
Your dreams            be dreams,            be dreams.
```

F-Stop Blues

Words and Music by Jack Johnson

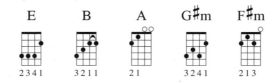

Verse 1

    E   B

     Hermit crabs and cow - ry shells

              |A

Crush be - neath his feet as he comes towards you.

     |E   B |A

He's   wav - ing at you.

       |E   B |

Lift him   up to see what you can see.

A

     He begins his focusing.

    |E   B |

He's   aim - ing at you.

A |E   B

     And now he has cutaways from mem - ories

    |A |

And   close-ups of anything that

E   B |

     He has seen or e - ven dreamed.

A

     And now he's finished focusing.

    |E   B |

He's   imagining lightning

A |

     Striking sea sickness

E   B |A   ‖

     Away from here.

Chorus

```
        E                    G♯m
        Look who's laughing now,

              |A        B        |
        That you've   wast - ed,

        E              G♯m           |A            B           |
        How many years?    And you've barely even tast - ed

        E              G♯m           |
        Anything remote - ly close to

        A                    B           |
        Everything you've boast - ed about.

        E                    G♯m        |A      B    ‖
        Look who's crying now.
```

Verse 2

```
        E                    B                |
          Driftwood floats after years of erosion.

        A                                    |
        Incoming tide touches roots to expose them.

        E                    B            |
          Quicksand steals my   shoes.

        A                            |
          Clouds bring the f-stop blues.

        F♯m              |A              ‖
```

Repeat Chorus

Fall Line

Words and Music by Jack Johnson

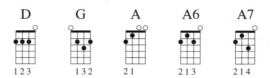

Verse 1

D
    And by the way, you know that hope will make you strange,

 |D
Make you blink, make you blank, make you sink.

     |G
It will make you a - fraid of change

  |G
And of - ten blame the box with the view of the world

G |D
   And the ones that fill the frame. I turn it up,

 |D
But then I turn it off, because I can't stand

D |G
When they start to talk about the hurting and killing.

   |G
Whose shoes are we filling? The damage and ruin, man,

 |G
The things that we're doing, God.

D
  We gotta stop, we gotta turn it all off;

  |D
We gotta rewind, (and) start it up again,

Chorus

```
           ‖A                   |A6              |
Because we fell across the fall    line.

A7                       |A6              |G         |           |
   Ain't there nothing sa - cred anymore?

               |G                |D      |G      |D      |G
Na, na, na,  na, na, na, na, na.
```

Verse 2

```
           ‖D                              |
Some - body saw him jump, yeah, but nobody saw him slip.

           |D                     |
I guess he lost a lot of hope, and then he lost his grip.

           |G                        |                    |
And now he's lying in the freeway in the middle of this mess.

G                        |              |
Guess we lost another one, just   like the other one.

D                      |
Optimistic hypocrite that didn't have the nerve to quit

   |D                              |
The things that kept him wanting more un - til he fin'lly reached the core.
```

Chorus

```
           ‖A                   |A6        |
He fell across the fall    line.

A7                     |A6              |G       |       |
   Ain't there nothing sa - cred anymore?

               |G                |D           ‖
Na, na, na,   na, na, na, na, na.
```

41

Flake

Words and Music by Jack Johnson

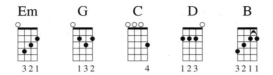

Verse 1

Em |G |
I know she said it's al - right,

C |G |
 But you can make it up next time.

Em |G |
I know she knows it's not right;

C |G |
 There ain't no use in ly - ing.

Em |G
Maybe she thinks I know something,

      |C |G |
Maybe, may - be she thinks it's fine.

Em |G
Maybe she knows something I don't.

    |C |D   ‖
I'm so, I'm so tired,   I'm so tired of trying.

Chorus

       G |D |
It seems to me that "may - be,"

Em |B |
It pretty much always means "no."

      |C |D |G |D |
So don't tell me you might; just let it go.

G |D |
And oftentimes we're la - zy;

Em |B
It seems to stand in my way.

     |C |D
'Cause no one, no, not no one

                    |G |D   ‖
Likes to be let down.

Verse 2

Em |G |
I know she loves the sun - rise,

C |G |
No longer sees it with her sleeping eyes and…

Em |G
I know that when she said she's gonna try,

      |C |G |
Well, it might not work because of other ties and….

Em |G |
I know she usually has some other ties, and

C |G |
I wouldn't want to break 'em, nah, I wouldn't want to break 'em.

Em |G
Maybe she'll help me to untie this,

     |C |D   ‖
But until then, well, I'm gonna have to lie, too.

Repeat Chorus

```
G                               |D         |
...It seems to me that "may - be,"

  Em                            |B
    It pretty much always means "no."

        |C          |D            |G       |D
So don't  tell me you might; just let it go.
```

Outro
```
        ||G                                   |C
(The) harder that you try, baby, the further you'll fall,

        |G                  |D        |
Even with all  the money in the whole  wide world.

G                               |
Please, please, please don't pass me...

C                               |
Please, please, please don't pass me...

D          C                    |G
Please, please, please don't pass me by.

        |G                                    |C
Everything you know about me now, baby, you gonna have to change,

                |G                  |D          |
You gonna have to call  it by a brand-new name,  oo, oo, oo.

G                               |
Please, please, please don't drag me...

C                               |
Please, please, please don't drag me...

D          C                    |G
Please, please, please don't drag me down.

        |G                                    |C
Just like a tree  down by the water, baby, I shall not move,

        |G                  |D          |
Even after all the silly things you do, oo, oo, oo,

G                               |
Please, please, please don't drag me...

C                               |
Please, please, please don't drag me...

D          C                    |G       |        ||
Please, please, please don't drag me down.
```

From the Clouds

Words and Music by
Jack Johnson

G   C   D   Am

Intro
    G |C   D |G |C   D |

    G |C   D |G |C   D

Verse 1
         ‖G
Oh,   you're such a pretty thing;
  |C   D |G |C   D
I'll take you and I'll make you all mine.
        |G
I would steal you from this patient world.
  |C   D |G |C   D
Let it   chase us; it could never take   you back.

Chorus 1
         ‖Am
We could watch it from the clouds.
    |Am |G |C   D
We can't stop it anyhow. It's not ours.
    |Am
We could watch it from the clouds.
    |Am |G |C
We can't stop it anyhow. It's not ours.
   D |G |C   D |G |C   D |
It's not ours.
    G |C   D |G |C   D   ‖

Verse 2

```
        G                                    |C
            And I know you know me well e - nough
                           D      |G         |C        D
To know I'm luck - y to have you.
           |G
But, oh,  it's just the little things,
             |C                   D     |G            |C        D
The words   that I should tell you all   the time.
           |G                        |
Like "you're so sweet to me"
C                          D     |G            |C      D         |
    When you beat me in double solitaire.
G                   |C                    D    |G          |C        D
You're so sweet to me   in a world that's not always fair.
```

Chorus 2

```
            ||Am
We could watch it from the clouds.
            |Am                     |G            |C        D
We can't stop it anyhow. It's not ours.
            |Am
We could watch it from the clouds.
            |Am                     |G            |C        D
We can't stop it anyhow. It's not ours.
```

Bridge

‖**C** |
The more love that you feel,

|**D** |
The more your little heart will ache.

|**C** |
Love's the only thing that carries on.

|**D** |
It's the only thing this world can't take.

                 |**G** |**C**
This love is ours.

           D |**G** |**C**
This love is ours.

Outro

           D   ‖**G** |
This love is… Oo,

C   **D** |**G** |**C**
  Oo, oo, oo,   oo, oo,   oo, oo.

           D |**G** |
This love is… Oo,

C   **D** |**G** |**C**   **D**
  Oo, oo, oo,   oo, oo,   oo, oo.

    |**G**
Oh, you're such a pretty thing;

|**C**   **D** |**G**   ‖
I'll take you and I'll make you all mine.

Fortunate Fool

Words and Music by Jack Johnson

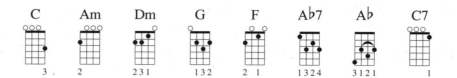

Verse 1

C   Am |C   Am |
She's got it all   figured out;

C   Am |C   Am |
She knows what ev - 'rything's about.

C   Am |Dm
And when   anybody doubts   her

          |G |Dm   G
Or sings songs without   her,

            |C   Am |C   Am ||
She's just so… Mm.

Verse 2

C   Am |C   Am |
She knows the world   is just her stage,

C   Am |C   Am |
And so she'll nev - er misbehave.

C   Am |Dm
She gives thanks   for what they gave   her.

           G |Dm   G
Man, they practic'lly made   her

        |C   Am |C   Am
Into a… Mm.

       |F
But she's the one that stumbles when she talks about

       |G
The seven foreign films that she's checked out.

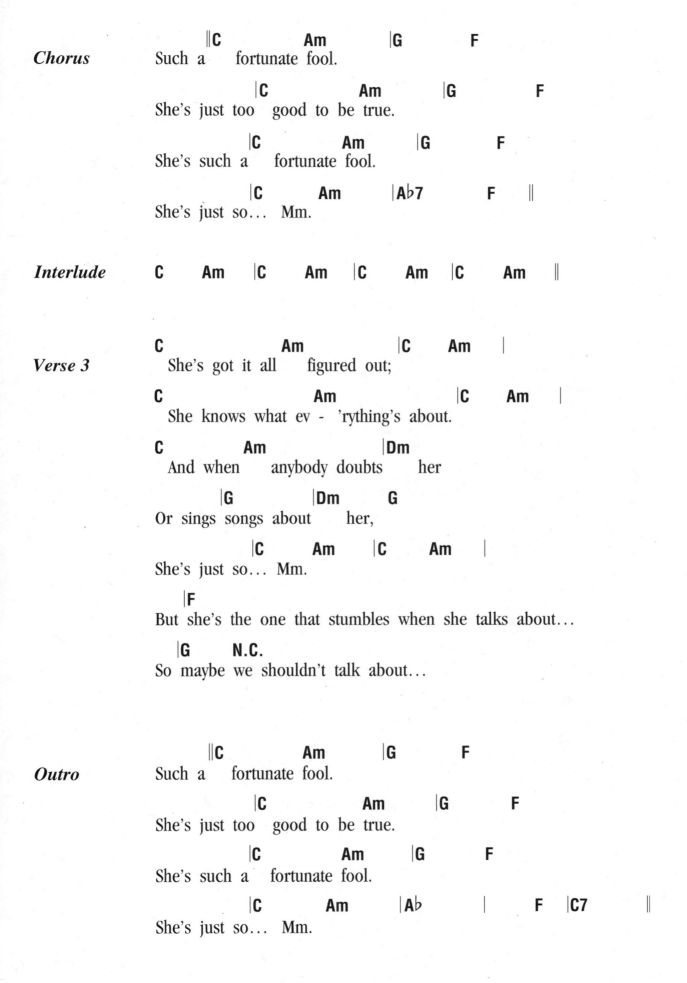

Chorus

```
              ‖C          Am         |G          F
Such a    fortunate fool.
                     |C           Am          |G           F
She's just too  good to be true.
                  |C          Am         |G           F
She's such a    fortunate fool.
                  |C          Am     |A♭7        F      ‖
She's just so… Mm.
```

Interlude

```
C     Am    |C     Am    |C     Am    |C     Am     ‖
```

Verse 3

```
C                   Am           |C    Am     |
  She's got it all     figured out;
C                  Am              |C    Am      |
  She knows what ev - 'rything's about.
C        Am              |Dm
  And when    anybody doubts      her
        |G          |Dm      G
Or sings songs about      her,
               |C     Am    |C     Am     |
She's just so… Mm.
   |F
But she's the one that stumbles when she talks about…
   |G       N.C.
So maybe we shouldn't talk about…
```

Outro

```
            ‖C         Am        |G         F
Such a    fortunate fool.
           |C           Am         |G          F
She's just too  good to be true.
           |C          Am       |G      F
She's such a    fortunate fool.
           |C         Am       |A♭       |      F  |C7          ‖
She's just so… Mm.
```

49

Gone

Words and Music by Jack Johnson

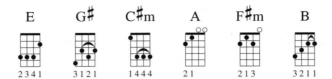

Verse 1

<pre>
E   G# |C#m   A |
Look at all those fancy clothes.

E   G# |C#m   A |
But these could keep us warm   just like those.

E   G# |C#m   A |
And what about your soul?   Is it cold?   Is it

F#m |B ||
      Straight from the mold and ready to be sold?
</pre>

Verse 2

<pre>
E   G# |C#m   A |
And cars and phones and diamond rings;   bling, bling.

E   G# |C#m   A |
Those are only remov - able things.

E   G# |C#m   A |
And what about your mind?   Does it shine   or

F#m |B ||
   Are there things that concern you   more than your time?
</pre>

Chorus

   E   B |C#m   A
  Gone, going, gone,   everything gone.

     |E   B |C#m   A
Give a damn. Gone be the birds when they don't want to sing.

     |E   B |C#m   A |E C#m |E C#m ||
Gone people, all awkward with their things. gone.

Verse 3

 E   G# |C#m   A |
  Look at you, out to make a deal.

 E   G# |C#m   A |
  You try to be appealing, but you lose your appeal.

 E   G# |C#m   A
  And what about those shoes   you're in today?

            |F#m |B ||
They'll do no good   on the bridges you burnt along the way, oh.

Chorus

 E   B |C#m   A |
  You're willing to sell   anything. Gone with your herd.

 E   B |C#m   A
  Leave your footprints (and) we'll shame them with our words.

     |E   B |C#m   A ||
Gone people,   all careless and con - sumed. Gone.

Chorus

 E   B |C#m   A
  Gone, going, gone,   everything gone.

    |E   B |C#m   A
Give a damn. Gone be the birds if they don't wanna sing.

     |E   B |C#m   A |E ||
Gone people, all awkward with their things. Gone.

Good People

Words and Music by Jack Johnson

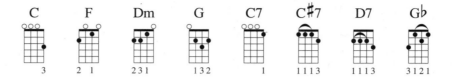

Verse 1

C   F |Dm
Well, you win; it's your show   now.

G |
So what's it gonna be?

C   F |
'Cause people   will tune in.

Dm   G |
How many train wrecks do we need to see

C   F |
Before   we lose touch?

Dm   G |
Oh, and we thought this was low.

C   F |Dm
Well, it's bad, gettin' worse,   oh.

Chorus

```
          G                      ‖C      F      |
          Where'd all the good people go?

Dm                  G
          I've been changing channels;

            |C                    F            |
I don't     see them on the T - V shows.

Dm      G                        |C    F      |
          Where'd all the good people go?

Dm            G                  |C      F    |Dm    G
          We got heaps and heaps of what  we sow.
```


Verse 2

```
            ‖C                  F
They got this and that with a rattle a tat.

          |Dm                G
Testing,     one, two. Man, what - cha gonna do?

          |C                 F            |
Bad news, misused, got too much to lose.

Dm                          G
Gimme some truth. Now who's  side are we on?

          |C          F
What - ever you say.

            |Dm              |G
Turn on the boob tube; I'm in the mood to obey.

  |C              F
So  lead me astray.

              |Dm
And by the way     now...
```


Repeat Chorus

Bridge

F |C7   C♯7 |
Sitting 'round, feeling far away.   Yeah.

D7 |G
So far away, but I can feel the de - bris.

               G♭ |
Can you feel it?

F |C7   C♯7 |
You interrupt me from a friendly conversation

D7 |G   G♭ |
To tell me how great it's all gonna be.

F |C7   C♯7
You might no - tice some hesitation,

       |D7
'Cause   it's important to you;

                |G
It's not important to me.

             G♭ |
Mm, mm, mm, mm.

F |C7   C♯7 |
Way down by the edge of your reason,

D7
Well, it's beginning to show,

   |F
And all I really wanna know is...

Repeat Chorus

Verse 3

```
      ‖C                    F
They got this and that with a rattle a tat.

        |Dm                 G
Testing,    one, two. Man, what - cha gonna do?

      |C            F
Bad news, misused,  give me some truth.

         |Dm
You got too much to lose.

        G                  |C
Who's  side are we on today,  anyway?

                  F              |
Okay, what - ever you say,

Dm                      G              |
Wrong or resolute but in the mood to obey.

C            F          |Dm         G          |
Station to sta - tion, desensi - tizing the na - tion.

C                    ‖
Going, going, gone.
```

Holes to Heaven

Words and Music by Jack Johnson

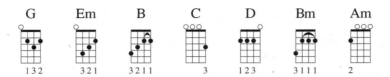

Verse 1

|G
The air was more than human

|G
And the heat   was more than hungry,

|G |Em |
And the cars   were square and spitting diesel fumes.

|G
The bulls were running wild

|G
Because they're big and mean and sacred,

|G |Em |
And the chil - dren were playing cricket with no shoes.

Pre-Chorus

‖B | |
The next morning we woke up, man, with a seven-hour drive.

C
There we were stuck in Port Blaire,

|C   ‖
Where boats break and children stare.

Chorus

G   D
There were so many fewer questions

  |Em   Bm |C Bm |Am
When stars were still just the holes to heav - en. Mm, hmm.

  |G   D
And there were so many fewer questions

  |Em   Bm |C Bm
When stars were still just the holes to heav - en.

  |Am |G | | | ‖
Mm.   Mm, mm.

Verse 2

G
Disembarking from the port,

  |G |
With no mistakes of any sort.

G |Em |
Moving south, the engine running smooth.

  |G
Of - ficials were quite friendly

     |G
Once we drowned them with our sweet talk

    |G |Em |
And we bribed them with our cigarettes and booze.

Pre-Chorus

  ‖B | |
The next morning we woke up, man, with the sunrise to the right,

C
Moving back north to Port Blaire,

  |C   ‖
Where boats break and children stare.

Repeat Chorus

The Horizon Has Been Defeated

Words and Music by Jack Johnson

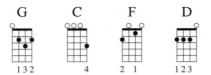

Verse 1

|G   C
(The) ho - rizon has been defeat - ed

|F   G |
By the pirates of the new age.

G   C
Alien casi - nos,

|F   G
Well, maybe it's just time to say

|G   C
That things can go bad

|F   G
And make you want to run away.

|G |C
But as we grow old - er,

|F |D | ||
The trouble just seems to   stay.

Verse 2

     G   C
Future complica - tions

       |F   G
In the strings between the cans.

      |G   C
But no prints can come from fin - gers

       |F   G
If ma - chines become our hands.

         |G   C
And then our feet become the wheels,

        |F   G
And then the wheels become the cars.

        |G   C
And then the rigs begin to drill

      |F |D | ||
Until the drilling goes too   far.

Chorus

     G   C
Things can go bad

      |F   G
And make you want to run away.

     |G   C
But as we grow old - er,

      |F |D   C |G |D   C |G ||
(The) ho - rizon begins to   fade, fade, fade,   fade away.

Verse 3

G   C |
Thingamajigsaw puz - zled;

F   G |
Anger, don't you step too close.

     |G
'Cause people are lonely

      C |F   G |
And on - ly ani - mals with fancy shoes.

G   C |
Hallelujah zig zag noth - ing;

F   G
Misery, it's on the loose.

     |G
'Cause people are lonely

      C |F |
And on - ly ani - mals with too many tools

D |
That can build all the junk that we sell.

D   ‖
Oh, sometime, man, make you want to yell, and….

Chorus

G   C
Things can go bad

     |F   G
And make you want to run away.

     |G   C
But as we grow old - er,

            |F |D C |G |D C |G |
(The) ho - rizon begins to fade away,   fade   away.

D   C |G |
Fade, fade, fade.

D   C |G   ‖
Fade, fade, fade.

If I Had Eyes

Words and Music by
Jack Johnson

D   A   G   Em

1 2 3   2 1   1 3 2   3 2 1

Intro
|D |A |G |Em |
|D |A |G |Em ||

Verse 1

   D |A
If I had eyes in the back of my head,
       |G |Em |
I would have told you that you looked good as I walked away.
   D |A |G |Em

Verse 2

    ||D |A
And if you could have tried to trust the hand that fed,
       |G |Em |
You would have never been hungry but you'd never really be.
   D |A |G |Em ||

Verse 3

   D |A
More of this or less of this or is there any difference?
   |G |Em
Or are we just holding onto the things
       |A |
That we don't have any - more?

Chorus 1

```
         ‖D              Em  |G              D
Sometimes time doesn't heal. No, not at all.
    |D           Em    |G          D           |
It just stands still    while we fall.
D         Em             |G           D         |            Em
In or out    of love a - gain, I doubt   I'm gonna win you back
                    |G          D                    |A          |
When you've got eyes like that,   that won't let me in.
A                    |D         |A           |G           |Em             |
  Always looking out.          Oo,      oo, oo, oo, oo.
D          |A         |G         |Em
Oo,      oo,       oo, oo, oo, oo.
```

Verse 4

```
         ‖D                    |A                    |
A lot of people spend their time just floating.
G                    |Em             |
We were victims, to - gether but lonely.
D                          |A
You've got hungry eyes that just can't look forward.
    |G                      |Em                  |
Can't give them enough, but we just can't start over.
D                          |A          |
Building with bent nails, we're falling but holding.
G                      |Em              |A         |
I don't want to take up any more of your time.    Time,   time, time.
```

62

Chorus 2

```
                    ‖D              Em  |G                  D
Sometimes  time  doesn't  heal.  No,  not  at  all.
     |D          Em     |G            D              |
It  just  stands  still      while  we  fall.
D          Em            |G              D              |            Em
In  or  out      of  love  a - gain,  I  doubt    I'm  gonna  win  you  back
                    |G              D                      |A              |
When  you've  got  eyes  like  that,    that  won't  let  me  in.
A                        |D        |A              |G                  |
  Always  looking  out.          Oo,        oo,  oo,  oo,  oo.
```

Outro

```
Em                          ‖D        |A                  |G              |
  Always  looking… Oo,        oo,        oo,  oo,  oo,  oo.
Em                      |D        |A                  |G              |
  Always  looking    out.        oo,        oo,  oo,  oo,  oo.
Em                      |D        |A                  |G              |
  Always  looking    out.        oo,        oo,  oo,  oo,  oo.
Em                      |D              ‖
  Always  looking    out.
```

If I Could

Words and Music by Jack Johnson

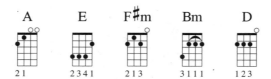

Verse 1

    A   **E**   **|F♯m**
    A brand-new baby was born yesterday

Bm   **|A**   **E**   **|F♯m Bm**   **|**
    Just in time.

A   **E**   **|**
    Papa cried,   baby cried,

F♯m   **Bm**   **|A**   **E**   **|F♯m Bm**   **|**
    Said, "Your tears   are like mine."

A   **E**   **|F♯m**
    I heard some words from a friend on the phone;

Bm   **|A**   **E**   **|F♯m Bm**   **|**
    Didn't sound so good.

A   **E**   **|F♯m**
    The doctor gave him two weeks to live;

Bm   **|E**   **||**
    I'd give him more   if I could.

```
                A    D  |Bm    E                     |A    D        |
Chorus                     You  know  that  I  would    now,

                Bm      E          |A      D      |
                   If  only  I  could.

                Bm        E               |A    D      |
                   You  know  that  I  would    now,

                Bm      E               ‖
                   If  only  I  could.


Interlude       A     E    |F♯m   Bm   |A    E    |F♯m   Bm      ‖


                A                E            |F♯m
Verse 2            Down  the  mid - dle  drops  one  more

                Bm                |A    E    |F♯m   Bm
                   Grain  of  sand.

                          |A                E              |F♯m  Bm        |A    E  |F♯m Bm |
                They  say  that  new  life  makes  losing  life  eas - ier   to  under - stand.

                A              E            |F♯m
                   Words  are  kind;  they  help  ease      the  mind.

                    Bm          |A    E    |F♯m   Bm
                I'll  miss  my  old  friend.

                          |A            E
                And  though  you've    gotta  go,

                          |F♯m                Bm
                We'll  keep  a  piece  of  your  soul.

                          |E                        ‖
                One  goes  out,        one  comes  in.



Repeat Chorus
```

65

Inaudible Melodies

Words and Music by Jack Johnson

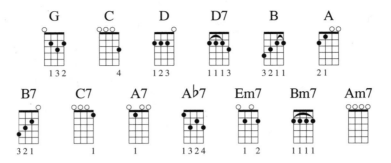

Verse 1

|G
Brushfire fairytales,

|C
Itsy bitsy diamond whales.

|G
Big fat hurricanes,

|C
Yellow-bellied given names.

|D
Well, shortcuts can slow you down.

|C
And in the end   we're bound

|G |D
To rebound off of we.

Verse 2

          ‖**G**
Well, dust off your thinking caps,

       |**C**
Solar powered plastic plants.

        |**G**
Pretty pictures of things we ate,

        |**C**
We are only what   we hate.

       |**D**
But in the long run we have found

      |**C**
Silent films are full of sound,

   |**G** |**D7**   ‖
Inaudibly free.

Chorus

G
Slow down, everyone,

  |**B** |
You're moving too fast.

C
Frames can't catch you when

  |**A**   ‖
You're moving like that.

Bridge 1

        G
Inaudible melodies

       |**B** |
Serve narrational strategies.

        C
Unobtrusive tones

           |**A**
Help to notice nothing but the zone

       |**G** |
Of visual relevancy.

B |
Frame-lines tell me what to see,

C
Chopping like an axe,

         |**A**   ‖
Or maybe Eisenstein should just relax.

Repeat Chorus

Bridge 2

        ‖**G**
Well, Plato's cave is full of freaks

        |**B7**
De - manding refunds for the things they've seen.

    |**C7**
I wish they could believe

            |**A7**   **A♭7**   ‖
In all the things   that never made the screen. And just

Repeat Chorus

Outro   **G**   **D7** |**Em7**   **Bm7** |**C**   **Bm7** |**Am7** |**G**   ‖

Losing Hope

Words and Music by Jack Johnson

Am   C   G   F   D

Verse 1

               |Am   **C**   **G**
I got a faulty parachute. I got a stranger's friend,

               |Am   **C**   **G**
An ex - citing change in my butcher's blend,

             |Am   **C**   **G**
A symbol on the ceiling with the flick of a switch,

               |Am   **C**   **G**   **|F**   **|**
Yeah, my new-found hero in the enemy's ditch,   yeah.

Verse 2

               ‖Am   **C**   **G**
Well, somebody's something was left in the room,

             |Am   **C**   **G**
And now that it's gone, well, of course   we assume

             |Am   **C**   **G**
That somebody else needed some - thing so bad,

             |Am   **C**   **G**   **|F**   **|**   **‖**
They took ev'rything that somebody had.

Chorus

```
          C            G       |Am              |
          Losing  hope    is eas -  y

          D                        G
          When  your  only  friend    is  gone,

              |D                   G             |
          And  every  time  you  look    around,

          D                    G                  |C      C/B      |
            Well,  it  all,  it  all   just  seems  to  change.
          |Am       C   G  |Am      C   G  |Am      C   G  |Am       C   G
```


Verse 3

```
              ||Am                      C           G
          The  mark  was  left;  man,  it's  nev - er  the  same.

                  |Am                    C               G         |
          Next  time     that  you  shoot,  make  sure  that  you  aim.

          Am                    C        G
          Open  windows  with  pass - ing  cars,

           |Am                    C   G  |F         |            ||
          A  brand-new  night  with  the  same  old  stars.
```


Repeat Chorus

Verse 4

```
         G        ‖Am    C   G       |Am
         Feed the fool       a piece of the pie.

         C        G         |Am       C        G            |Am
         Make a fool of his sys - tem.     Make a fool of his mind.

         C        G         |Am  C    G        |Am
         Give him bottles of lies,      and maybe he'll    find

         C    G        |Am       C            G       |Am      C  G |F   |       ‖
         His place in heav - en,     because he might just die.
```

Repeat Chorus

```
              |C       G       |Am             |
         … But hanging on    is eas - y,

         D                     G
         When you've got a friend   to call.

              |D            G          |
         When nothing's making sense at all,

         D                    G                  |C     C/B      |
           You're not the only one   who's afraid of change.

         Am    C  G  |Am    C  G  |Am    C  G  |Am    C  G  |Am         ‖
```

Middle Man

Words and Music by Jack Johnson

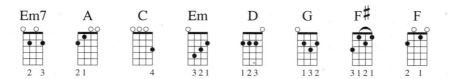

Verse 1

|**Em7**
Well, he's not necessarily trying to say that he minds it,

|**A**
But someone plays evil tricks on that kid.

|**Em7**
Yeah, he's not necessarily trying to say God can't be trusted,

|**A**
Yeah, but someone plays evil tricks on that kid.

|**Em7**
And certain situations scream for deviations,

|**A**
But somehow he always gets stuck in the middle

|**Em7**
Of this and that and, man, he should try less

|**A**
Every time he's rejected, man, he loses affection.

|**C**
But don't we all, don't we just got to give a little time?

A   **D**
Maybe give a friend a call instead of making him

Chorus

        ‖**Em**   **D** |
Con - fused.

A   **D** |**Em**   **D** |
What a terrible thing for you to do.

A   **D** |**Em**   **D** |
What an awful thing for you to say.

A   **D** |**A** |**G**   **F♯**   **F** |
What a terrible thing for you to re - lay.

Em |**A** |**Em** |**A**

Verse 2

        ‖**Em7**
Well, I know some peoples, they got a little less than nothing,

        |**A** |
Yeah, but still find some to spare

Em7 |
And other people got more than they could use,

A |
But they don't share.

Em7
And some people got problems, man,

        |**A** |
They got awful complications.

Em7 |**A**
Other people got perfect situa - tions

With no provocation.

      |**C** |
But don't we all, don't we just got to give a little time?

A   **D**
Maybe give a friend a call instead of making him

Chorus

```
       ‖Em           D          |
       Con - fused.

       A                  D                |Em    D      |
       What a terrible thing for you to do.

       A                  D                |Em    D      |
       What an awful thing for you to say.

       A                  D
       What a terrible thing for you.

                  |Em    D      |
       Confused.

       A                  D                |Em    D      |
       What a terrible thing for you to do.

       A                  D                |Em    D      |
       What an awful thing for you to say.

       A                  D                |A         |G    F♯    F    |
       What a terrible thing for you to re - lay.

       Em        |A        |Em        |A
```

Outro

```
       ‖Em            |
       Con - fused.

       A                              |Em        |A
       What an awful thing for you to do.

       |Em           |
       Con - fused.

       A                              |Em      |A        |Em        ‖
       What an awful thing for you to say.
```

Mudfootball
(For Moe Lerner)

Words and Music by Jack Johnson

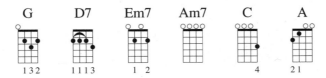

Verse 1

G
Saturday morning and it's time to go.

G
One day these could be the days, but who could have known?

D7
Loading in the back of a pickup truck.

D7
Riding with the boys and pushing the luck.

G
Singing songs loud on the way to the game.

G
Wishing all the things could still be the same.

D7
Chinese homeruns over the backstop.

|**D7**
Ko - kua on the ball, and soda pop. Well…

Chorus

Em7   Am7
    We used to laugh a lot,

|C
But only because we thought

     |G   D7 |G   D7 |
That ev - 'rything good always would remain.

G   D7 |G   D7 |
Nothing's gonna change; there's no need to complain.

G | |D7 | ||

Verse 2

G
Sunday morning and it's time to go.

     |G |
Been raining all night so ev'rybody knows.

D7
Over to the field for tackle football.

       |D7 |
Big hits,   big hats, yeah, give me the ball.

G |
Rain is pouring, touchdown scoring.

G |
Keep on rolling, never boring.

D7
Karma, karma, karma chameleon.

     |D7 ||
We're talking kinda funny from helium. Well,

Repeat Chorus

Verse 3

G

Monday morning and it's time to go.

G

Wet trunks and schoolbooks and sand on my toes.

|D7

Do an - ything you can to dodge the bus stop blues,

|D7

Like driving a padiddle with a burnt-out fuse.

|G

Well, my best friend, Kimi, wants to go with you,

|G

So meet her by the sugar mill after school.

|D7

My best friend, Kimi, wants to go with you,

D7

Meet her by the sugar mill after school. Well,

Chorus

Em7   Am7

   We used to laugh a lot,

|C

But only because we thought

    |G   D7 |G   D7

That ev - 'rything good always would remain.

Em7   Am7

   We used to laugh a lot,

|C

But only because we thought

    |A

That ev - 'rything good always would,

 |C |G   D7

Ev - 'rything good always would remain.

    |G   D7 |G

Mm.

Never Know

Words and Music by Jack Johnson

Em7   Am7   D7   G   Gmaj7   C

Intro   **Em7** |**Am7** |**D7** |**G**   **Gmaj7** ‖

Verse 1

Em7
I heard this old story before,

|**Am7**
Where the people keep on killing for their metaphors

|**D7** |**G**   **Gmaj7**
But   don't leave much up to the i - magina - tion.

|**Em7**
So I   wanna give this imagery back,

|**Am7**
But I   know it just ain't so easy like that.

|**D7**
So   I turn the page and read the story

|**G**   **Gmaj7** |**C**
A - gain and a - gain and a - gain.

|**Am**
Sure seems the same

With a different name.

|**D7**
We're breaking and rebuilding

|**D7**
And we're growing, always guessing.

Chorus

‖Em7   Am7
Never know - ing;

|D7   G
Shock - ing, but we're noth - ing.

|Em7 Am7
We're just mo - ments;

|D7 |G
We're clev - er but we're clue - less.

|Em7 Am7
We're just hu - man,

|D7   G
Amus - ing and confus - ing.

|Em7 Am7 |D7   G
We're try - ing, but where is this all lead - ing?

|Em7 |Am7 |D7 |G
We'll never know.

Verse 2

           ‖**Em7**
It all happened so much   faster than you could say "disaster."

     |**Am7**
Wanna take a time lapse and look at it backwards,

    |**D7**
Find the last word?

           |**G**   **Gmaj7**
And maybe that's just the answer that we're after.

      |**Em7**
But after all, we're just a bubble in a boiling pot,

    |**Am7**
Just one breath in a chain of thought.

    |**D7**
We're moments just combusting;

   |**G**   **Gmaj7** |**C**
Feel certain but we'll never, never know.

        |**Am**
Sure seems the same.

Give it a diff'rent name.

    |**D7**
We're begging and we're needing

    |**D7**
And we're trying and we're breathing.

Chorus

```
     ‖Em7    Am7
Never  know - ing;

        |D7                    G
Shock - ing,  but  we're  noth - ing.

            |Em7   Am7
We're  just  mo - ments;

           |D7                    G
We're  clev - er  but  we're  clue - less.

              |Em7 Am7
We're  just  hu   -   man,

        |D7              G
Amus - ing  and confus - ing.

            |Em7  Am7         |D7                    |G
We're  help  -  ing,  we're  build - ing  and  we're  grow - ing.

              |Em7                          |
Never  know.      You  can  never  know,

Am7                  |D7              |G           ‖
   Never  know,        never  know.
```

Verse 3

Em7
     Knock, knock, comin' door to door;

Am7
Tell ya that their metaphor's better than yours.

 |D7
And you can either sink or swim;

G
Things are looking pretty grim.

 |Em7 |Am7
If you don't believe in what they're spoon - feeding,

    |D7
It's got no feeling,

          |G   Gmaj7 |C
So I read it again and a - gain and a - gain.

Sure seems the same.

Am7
   So many different names

 |D7
Our hearts are strong; our heads are weak.

 |D7
We'll always be competing.

Chorus

```
    ‖Em7      Am7
Never  know - ing;

      |D7                    G
Shock - ing,  but  we're  noth - ing.

         |Em7    Am7
We're  just  mo -  ments;

         |D7                  G
We're  clev - er  but  we're  clue - less.

            |Em7    Am7
We're  just  hu  -    man,

       |D7                G
Amus -  ing  and confus - ing.

            |Em7  Am7    |D7              G
But  the  truth      is,   all   we  got  is  ques - tions.

                 |Em7                          |
We'll  never  know.        You  can  never  know,

Am7                    |D7              |G          ‖
  Never  know,      never  know.
```


Outro   Em7 |Am7 |D7 |G |Em7   ‖

No Other Way

Words and Music by Jack Johnson

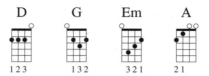

Verse 1

D
When your mind is a mess,   so is mine.   I can't sleep,

G
'Cause it hurts when I think.   My thoughts aren't at peace

Em
With the plans that we make,   chances we take.

G
They're not yours; they're not mine.   There's waves that can break.

D
All the words that we said   and the words that we mean.

G
Words can fall short,   can't see the unseen.

Em
'Cause the world is awake.

|**G**
For somebody's sake   now, please close your eyes.

G
Woman, please get some sleep.

Chorus

```
     D                       |A            G
       And  know  that  if  I  knew  all  of  the  answers,
          |D                          |
     I would    not   hold  them  from  you.
     A          G                    |
     Know  all  the  things  that  I  know;
     D                       |A         G        |Em        |
        We  told  each  other    there  is  no  other   way.
            |G        |         ||
     Mm,  mm,    mm.
```

Verse 2

```
     D                          |
        Well,  too  much  silence  can  be    misleading.
          |G                          |
     You're  drifting;  I  can  hear  it  in  the  way  that  you're  breathing.
        |Em                     |
     We   don't  really  need  to  find  rea - son,
                            |G
     'Cause  out  the  same  door   that  it  came,
            |G              |
     Well,  it's  leav - ing,  it's   leaving.
     D                          |
     Leaving  like  a  day  that's  done  and  part  of  a  season.
        |G                        |
     Re - solve  is  just  a  concept  that's  as  dead  as  the  leaves,
            |Em                  |
     But  at  least     we  can  sleep.     It's  all  that  we  need.
               |G
     When  we  wake   we  would  find,
        |G                              ||
     Our  minds  would  be  free  to  go  to  sleep.
```

Repeat Chorus

Posters

Words and Music by Jack Johnson

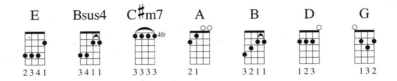

Verse 1

      E   Bsus4
Looking at himself but wishing he was someone else

         |C♯m7   Bsus4 |E Bsus4 |C♯m7 Bsus4
Because the posters on the wall, they don't look like him at all.

      |E   Bsus4 |
So he ties it up, he tucks it in, he pulls it back and gives a grin,

C♯m7   Bsus4 |E Bsus4 |C♯m7 Bsus4
Laughing at himself because he knows he ain't loved at all.

Chorus

           ||A
He gets his courage from the can; it makes him feel like a man,

        |B |E Bsus4 |C♯m7 Bsus4
Because he's loving all the ladies but the ladies don't love him at all.

       |A
'Cause when he's not drunk he's only stuck on himself,

       |B |E Bsus4 |C♯m7 Bsus4||
And then   he has the nerve to say he needs a decent girl.

Verse 2

```
       E                              Bsus4
Looking at herself but wishing she was someone else
```

```
         |C♯m7                    Bsus4              |E  Bsus4 |C♯m7  Bsus4
Because the body of the doll, it don't look like hers at all.
```

```
         |E                        Bsus4                            |
So she straps it on, she sucks it in, she throws it up and gives a grin,
```

```
C♯m7                         Bsus4           |E  Bsus4 |C♯m7  Bsus4
Laughing at herself because she knows she ain't that at all.
```

Chorus

```
      ‖A
All caught up in the trends; well, the truth began to bend
```

```
     |B                                      |E  Bsus4 |C♯m7  Bsus4
And the next thing you know, man, there just ain't no truth left at all.
```

```
            |A
'Cause when the pretty girl walks, she walks so proud,
```

```
     |B                                      |E  Bsus4 |C♯m7  Bsus4
And when the pretty girl laughs, oh man, she laughs so loud.
```

Bridge

```
      ‖E                D                    |
And if it ain't this, then it's that. As a matter of fact,
```

```
C♯m7                    B           |
   She hasn't had a day    to relax
```

```
E            D              |
Since she has lost her
```

```
C♯m7                |B       |E  Bsus4 |C♯m7 N.C. |E  Bsus4 |C♯m7  G    A
   Ability to think    clear - ly.
```

Verse 3

     ‖**E**   **Bsus4** |
Well, I'm an energetic hypothetic version of another person.

C♯m7   **Bsus4** |**E** **Bsus4** |**C♯m7** **Bsus4**
Check out my outsides; there ain't nothing in here.

     |**E**   **Bsus4** |
Well, I'm a superficial, systematic, music television addict.

C♯m7   **Bsus4**
Check out my outsides; there ain't nothing in…

Chorus

     ‖**A** |
Here   comes another one, just like the other one.

B
Looking at himself but wishing he was someone else

     |**E**   **Bsus4** |
Because the posters on the wall, they don't look like him.

C♯m7   **Bsus4** |
Ties it up, he tucks it in, he pulls it back and gives a grin,

E   **Bsus4** |
Laughing at himself because he knows he ain't loved at all.

C♯m7   **Bsus4** |**E**   ‖
     He knows he ain't loved at all.

Rodeo Clowns

Words and Music by Jack Johnson

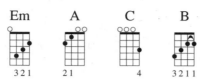

Verse 1

Em
Sweeping the floors, open up the doors, yeah.

A
Turn on the lights, getting ready for tonight.

C
Nobody's romancing 'cause it's too early for dancing,

|**B** ‖
But here comes the music.

Verse 2

Em
Bright lights flashing to cover up your lack of soul.

|**A**
Man - y people, so many problems,

|**C**
So many reasons to buy an - other round; drink it down.

|**B**
Just another night on the town

|**Em**
With the big man, money man, better than the other man.

A
He got the plan with the million dollar give a damn.

C
When nobody understands he'll become a smaller man.

|**B**
The bright lights keep flashing.

Chorus

‖**Em**   **B**

Women keep on dancing with the clowns, yeah, yeah, yeah.

                    |**C**   **A**

They pick me up when I'm down,   yeah, yeah.

           |**Em**   **B**

The rodeo clowns,   yeah, yeah, yeah,

                   |**C**   **A**   ‖

They pick me up when I'm down.

Verse 3

‖**Em**

The disco ball spinning,

                       |**A**

All the music and the women and the shots of tequila.

Man, they say that they need ya.

 |**C**

But what they really need

   |**B**

Is just a little room to breathe.

   |**Em**

Teeny bopping disco queen,

                  |**A**

She barely understands her dreams of bellybutton rings

             |**C**

And other kinds of things sym - bolic of change.

But the thing that is strange

  |**B**

Is that the changes occurred.

                                                    ‖Em   B
Chorus   And now she's just a part of the herd,   yeah, yeah, yeah.

                                            |C   A
                  Man, I thought that you heard, yeah, yeah.

                                    |Em   B
                  The changes occurred,   yeah, yeah, yeah.

                                    |C   A   ‖
                  Just a part of the herd.

                  Em |
Verse 4   Lights out, shut down, late night, wet ground.

                  A |
                   You walk by, look at him, but he can't look at you, yeah.

                  C |
                   You might feel pity, but he only feels the ground.

                  B |
                   You understand moods, but he only knows letdown.

                  Em |
                     By the corner there's another one

                  A |
                  Reaching out a hand, coming from a broken man.

                       |C |B
                  Well,   you try to live, but he's done trying.   Not dead,

                            ‖Em
Chorus   But definitely dying

                  B |C   A
                   With the rest of the clowns,   yeah, yeah.

                                    |Em   B
                  Mm, mm, mm, mm,   mm, mm, mm,

                                          |C   A   ‖
                  With the rest of the clowns.

Repeat Verse 1

Sexy Plexi

Words and Music by Jack Johnson

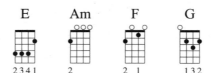

Verse 1

E |Am
Sexy, sexy, made up of plexi dis - asters.

E
Pushing and pulling, conservative rolling,

Am
Unlike plastic, easier to see through,

E
Just like glass with no ring,

Am
Softer and sadder you sing.

E
Sexy, sexy, do your thing,

Am
Learn to be shy and then you can sting.

E
Plexi, plexi, bend, don't shatter.

F   G
Once you're broken, shape won't matter.

Chorus

    Am   **G**
You're breaking your   mind

|**F**   **E**
By killing the time that kills   you.

  |**Am**   **G**
But you can't blame the time,

              |**F**   **E** |**Am** | ‖
'Cause it's on - ly in your mind.

Verse 2

    E
Quickly, quickly grow and then you'll know

         |**Am**
It's such an awkward show to see.

  |**E**
And everyone you wanted to know

  |**Am**
And everyone you wanted to meet

    |**E** |**Am**
Have all   gone away.

           |**E** |**F** **G**   ‖
Well, they've all   gone away.   And now…

Repeat Chorus

Bridge

  Am |**E**
You're breaking your mind, you're   breaking your mind.

    |**Am** |**E**
You're   breaking your mind, you're   breaking your mind.

    |**Am** |**E**
You're   breaking your mind, you're   breaking your mind.

    |**Am** |**E** |**F**   **G**   ‖
You're   breaking your mind, you're   breaking your mind, mind,   mind.

Outro   **Am**   **G** |**F**   **E** |**Am**   **G** |**F**   **E** |**Am**   ‖

Sitting, Waiting, Wishing

Words and Music by Jack Johnson

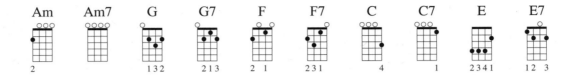

Verse 1

|Am   Am7 |
Well, I   was sitting, waiting, wishing

G   G7 |
You believed in superstitions;

F   F7 |C   C7
Then maybe you'd see the signs.

|Am   Am7
But Lord   knows that this world is cruel,

|G   G7
And I ain't the Lord, no, I'm just a fool,

|F   F7 |C   C7
Learning loving somebody don't make them love you.

Chorus

‖E   E7 |E   E7 |Am   Am7 |Am   Am7
Must I always   be wait - ing, wait - ing on you?

|E   E7 |E   E7 |Am   Am7 |Am   Am7
Must I always   be play - ing, play - ing your fool?

Verse 2

    ‖Am   Am7
I sang your songs, I danced your dance

   |G   G7 |
I gave your friends all a chance.

F   F7 |C   C7
Putting up with them wasn't worth never having you.

   |Am   Am7
Oh, maybe you've been through this before,

    |G   G7
But it's my first time, so please ignore

    |F   F7 |C   C7
The next few lines, 'cause they're directed at you.

Chorus

        ‖E   E7 |E   E7 |Am Am7 |Am Am7
I can't always   be wait - ing, wait - ing on you.

      |E   E7 |E   E7 |Am Am7 |Am Am7 ‖
I can't always   be play - ing, play - ing your fool.

Bridge

C |
I keep playing your part,

E |
But it's not my scene.

F |
Won't this plot not twist?

G   F |
I've had e - nough mystery.

C |
Keep building it up,

E |
But then you're shooting me down.

F |
But I'm already down;

G   ‖
Just wait a minute.

Interlude

Am   Am7 |G   G7 |
         Just sitting, waiting.

F   F7 |C   C7 |
         Just wait a minute.

Am   Am7 |G   G7 |
         Just sitting, waiting.

F   F7 |C   C7

Verse 3

‖Am   Am7
Well, if I was in your position,

|G   G7
I'd put down all my ammunition.

|F   F7 |C   C7
I'd wonder why it had taken me so long.

|Am   Am7
But Lord knows that I'm not you,

|G   G7
And if I was, I wouldn't be so cruel,

|F   F7 |C   C7
'Cause waiting on love ain't so easy to do.

Chorus

‖E   E7 |E   E7 |Am Am7 |Am Am7
Must I always   be wait - ing, wait - ing on you?

|E   E7 |E   E7 |Am Am7 |Am Am7
Must I always   be play - ing, play - ing your fool?

|E   E7 |E   E7 |Am Am7 |Am Am7
No, I can't always   be wait - ing, wait - ing on you.

|E   E7 |E   E7 |Am Am7 |E E7 |Am ‖
I can't always   be play - ing, play - ing your fool,   fool.   Mm, mm.

Taylor

Words and Music by Jack Johnson

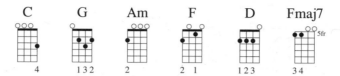

Verse 1

        |C   G |
They say Taylor was a good girl, never one to be late,

Am   F |C G |Am   F |
Complain, express ideas in her brain.

C   G
Working on the night shift, passing out the tickets;

       |Am   F |C G |Am   F
You're gonna have to pay her if you want to park here.

     |C   G |
Well, Mommy's little dancer has quite a little secret;

Am   F |C G |Am   F
Working on the streets now, never gonna keep it.

    |C   G
It's quite an imposition and now she's only wishing

    |Am   F |C G |Am F ||
That   she would have listened to the words they said.   Poor Taylor.

Chorus

```
        C          G              |Am         F             |
        She just wanders around,       unaf - fected by

        C          G              |Am   F                   |
        The winter winds, yeah,       and she'll pretend that

        C          G              |Am   F                   |
        She's somewhere else       so far and clear,

        C          G              |Am                       ||
        About  two thousand miles       from here.
```

Interlude

```
        C    G    |Am   F    |C    G    |Am   F    ||
```

Verse 2

```
        C                 G                      |Am        F
        Peter Patrick pit - ter patters on the win - dow,

         |C               G              |Am       F         |
        But Sunny Silhouette      won't let him     in.

        C                   G                    |Am          F
        Poor old Pete's got nothing 'cause he's been falling;

             |C              G              |Am        F
        Somehow Sunny knows   just where he's     been.

                           |C                    G          |Am    F    |
        He thinks that sing - ing on Sunday's gonna save his soul,

        C      G      |Am      F       |
        Now that Saturday's     gone.

        C                   G             |Am          F
        Sometimes he thinks     that he's on     his way,

                          |C      G    |Am
        But  I  could  see

                     F                   ||
        That his brake lights are on.
```

Chorus

```
        C        G          |Am      F         |
        He just wanders around,    unaf - fected by

        C        G          |Am      F                    |
        The winter winds, yeah,    and he'll pretend that

        C        G          |Am  F            |
        He's somewhere else   so far and clear,

        C        G              |Am               ‖
        About two thousand miles      from here.
```

Interlude   C   G |Am   F |C   G |Am   F

Verse 3

```
                        ‖C              G
        She's such a tough  enchilada filled   up with nada,

        |Am                        F               |C   G  |Am   F
        Giv - ing what she gotta give  to get a dollar bill.

                   |C                    G
        Used to be   a limber chicken; time's    a been a ticking.

           |Am                  F
        Now    she's finger licking to the man

               |C                    G
        With the money in his pocket, fly - ing in his rocket,

        |Am                    F                      |
        On - ly stopping by on his way to a better world.

        C   D  |F   G                    |
                 If Taylor finds a better world,

        C   D  |F      G                      |C          |Fmaj7    ‖
                 Then Taylor's gonna run away.
```

Staple It Together

Lyrics by Jack Johnson
Music by Jack Johnson and Merlo Podlewski

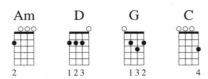

Verse 1

‖**Am**   **D**
It's really   too bad.

|**Am**   **D**
He became a pris - 'ner of his own past.

|**Am**   **D**
He stabbed a mo - ment in the back with a round thumbtack

|**Am**   **D**
That held   up the list of things he got to do.

|**Am**   **D**
It's really   no good.

|**Am**   **D**
He's moving on before he under - stood.

|**Am**   **D**
He shot the fu - ture in the foot with ev - 'ry step he took

|**Am**   **D**
From the places that he'd been 'cause he forgot to look.

Chorus

‖**Am**   **D** |
Better staple it together and call it bad weather.

G   **C** |
Staple it together and call it bad weather.

Am   **D** |
Staple it together and call it bad weather.

G   **C**
Staple it together and call it bad weather.

|**Am**   **D** |**Am**   **D** |**Am**   **D** |**Am**   **D**
Mm, mm.

Verse 2

         ‖**Am**   **D**
Well, I guess you could say

         |**Am**   **D**
That he don't even know where to be - gin.

            |**Am**   **D**
'Cause he looked   both ways, but he was so afraid,

        |**Am**   **D**
Diggin' deep into the ditch ev - 'ry chance he missed

          |**Am**   **D**
And the mess   he made.

      |**Am**   **D**
'Cause hate is such a strong word.

       |**Am**   **D**
And every brick he laid, a mis - take.

            |**Am**   **D**
They say that his walls   are getting taller, his world is getting smaller.

Repeat Chorus

Repeat Verse 1

Repeat Chorus

Outro

        ‖**Am**   **D** |
If the weather gets better, we should get together.

G   **C**
Spend a little time or we could do whatever.

    |**Am**   **D**
And if we get together we'd be twice as clever.

    |**G**   **C**
So, staple it together and call it bad weather.

      |**Am** **D** |**G** **C** |**Am** **D** |**G** **C** |**Am**   ‖
Mm, mm.

Times Like These

Words and Music by Jack Johnson

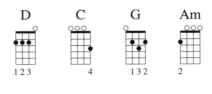

Intro   D |C |G |C |G

Verse 1
‖C
In times like   these,

|G
In times like   those,

|C
What will be will be,

|G
And so it goes.

|Am   D |
And it always goes on and on and on and on and on.

Am   D |
On and on and on and on and on it goes.

C |G
   Mm, hmm, hmm.

|C
Mm, hmm, hmm.

|G
Mm, hmm, hmm.

|Am
And there has always been laughing, crying, birth, and dying,

|D
Boys and girls with hearts that take and give and break,

|Am |D
And heal and grow and re-create and raise and nur - ture,

Verse 2　　　　But then hurt from time to times `‖C` like these,

`|G`
And times like　those.

`.|C`
What will be will be,

`|G`
And so it goes.

`|Am`
And there will always be stop and go and fast and slow

`|D`　　　　　　　　　　　　　　　　　　　　　　　　　　`|`
And action, re - action and sticks and stones and broken bones,

`Am`
Those for peace and those for war,

`|D`
And God bless these　ones, not those ones,

Verse 3

                               ‖C
But these ones made times like these,

                 |G
And times like   those.

                |C
What will be will be,

            |G
And so it goes.

                 |Am   D
And it always goes on and on and on and on and on.

        |Am   D |
And on   and on and on and on and on it goes.

C |G
    Mm, hmm, hmm.

          |C
Mm, hmm, hmm.

         |G
Mm, hmm, hmm.

              |Am |G
But somehow I   know it won't be the same.

              |Am |G   ‖
Somehow I   know (it'll) never be the same.

Tomorrow Morning

Words and Music by Jack Johnson

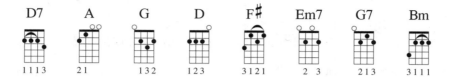

Intro

|D7 |
Well, that's all right, if that's all right.

A |G |
Two thousand miles, but still that's all right.

D7 | |
And that's all right, if that's all right.

A |G |D7 ‖
I'll see you in the morn - ing, if that's all right.

Verse 1

D F♯
What would you do if I wrote you a song?

|Em7 A
Would you give me some loving when I get home?

|D
Or would you be mad at me

F♯ |Em7
If I had a hard time getting a hold of you?

|G7 ‖
I try all the time.

Chorus

```
         D          Bm     |Em7                         A                          |D        Bm          |
         I'll bet that            you don't know any - body that could be    so bad.

         Em7                    A                              |D        Bm         |
             But if you did,     you'd be wondering where    I'm at.

         Em7                        A                          ‖
         I'll be home when to - morrow morning comes.
```

Interlude

```
         D        F♯      |Em7    A      |

         D        F♯      |Em7    A      ‖
```

Verse 2

```
         D                              F♯
         What would you do if I sang    you this song?

                  |Em7                      A
         The con - nection is bad, but that's only the phone.

                     |D
         'Cause when my words kiss your ear,

         F♯                       |Em7
         I'll be right there. The message is long,

                  |G7                      ‖
         'Cause baby, this is your song.
```

Chorus

```
          D           Bm  |Em7                      A                      |D        Bm      |
          I'll  bet,  bet            you  don't  know  any - body  that  could  be    so  bad.

          Em7                    A                        |D        Bm      |
            But  if  you  did,    you'd  be  wondering  where    I'm  at.

          Em7                      A
          I'll  be  home  when  to - morrow  morning…

              |D           Bm  |Em7                      A                      |D        Bm |
          And  I'll  bet,  bet            you  don't  know  any - body  that  could  be    so  bad.

          Em7                    A                        |D        Bm      |
            But  if  you  did,    you'd  be  wondering  where    I'm  at.

          Em7                      A                          |
          I'll  be  home  when  to - morrow  morning…

          D                    Bm
            And  that's  all  right,

              |Em7                      A                      |
          'Cause  I'll  be  home  when  to - morrow  morning…

          D              Bm
            And  that's  all      right,

              |Em7                      A                    |D            ‖
          'Cause  I'll  be  home  when  to - morrow  morning  comes.
```

Traffic in the Sky

Words and Music by Jack Johnson

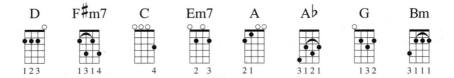

Verse 1

      D   **F♯m7**
There's traffic in the sky

                  |C   **Em7**
And it doesn't seem to be getting much better.

                 |D
There's kids playing games on the pavement,

        F♯m7   **|**
Drawing waves on the pavement, mm, hmm;

C   **Em7**   **|**
     Shadows of the planes on the pavement, mm, hmm.

D   **F♯m7**
 It's enough to make me cry,

                 |C   **Em7**
But that don't seem like it would make it feel better.

            |D
Maybe it's a dream and if I scream

       F♯m7
It will burst at the seams.

            |C   **Em7**
(The) whole place would fall into piec - es,

             |A   **A♭**   **||**
And then they'd say…

Chorus

      G   **A**
"Well, how could we have known?"

                      |D   **Bm**
I'll tell them it's not   so hard to tell.

        |G   **A**
No, no, no. If you keep adding stones,

                  |D   **Bm**
Soon the water will be lost in the well.

      |G   **A**   **‖**
Mm, hmm.

Verse 2

      D   **F♯m7**
Puzzle pieces in the ground;

     |C   **Em7**
No one ever seems to be digging.

              |D
Instead they're looking up towards the heavens

     F♯m7
With their eyes on the heavens, mm, hmm;

C   **Em7**
There're shadows on the way to the heavens, mm, hmm.

D   **F♯m7**
It's enough to make me cry,

       |C   **Em7**
But that don't seem like it would make it feel better.

           |D
The answers could be found.

             F♯m7
We could learn from digging down,

     |C   **Em7**
But no one ever seems to be dig - ging.

       |A   **A♭**   **‖**
Instead they'll say…

Repeat Chorus

Verse 3

```
        D                      F#m7
Words of wisdom all a - round,

        |C                 Em7
But no  one ever seems to listen.

                              |D
They're talking 'bout their plans on the paper,

        F#m7                              |
Building up    from the pavement, mm, hmm;

C                       Em7                        |
  There're shadows from the scrapers on the pavement, mm, hmm.

D                      F#m7
  It's enough to make me sigh,

        |C                          Em7
But that don't seem like it would make it feel better.

                     |D
The words are all a - round,

                    F#m7
But the words are only sounds,

        |C                 Em7
And no  one ever seems to lis - ten.

                |A              Ab  ‖
Instead, they'll say…
```

Chorus

```
G                                      A
"Well, how could we have known?"

                     |D              Bm
I'll tell them it's really not so hard to tell.

        |G                           A
No, no, no. If you keep adding stones,

                     |D              Bm
Soon the water will be lost in the well,

        |G       A        |D              ‖
Lost in the well. Mm,   mm, mm, mm.
```

110

Upside Down

from the Universal Pictures and Imagine Entertainment film CURIOUS GEORGE

Words and Music by
Jack Johnson

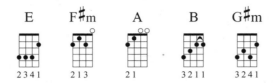

Intro

E | |F#m | |

E | |F#m | ||

Verse 1

E |
Who's to say   what's impossible?
|F#m |
But they forgot   this world keeps spinning.
|E | |F#m |
And with each new day   I can feel a change in everything.
F#m |E |
And as the surface breaks, re - flections fade.
E |F#m |
But in some ways they re - main the same.
F#m |E |
And as my mind begins to spread its wings,
E |F#m |
There's no stopping curi - osity.

```
                                      ‖E      F♯m              |
Chorus 1        I want to turn the whole thing upside    down.
                A           B                |E     F♯m          |
                  I'll find the things they say just can't be    found.
                A           B                |E    F♯m            |
                  I'll share this love I find with every - one.
                A           B                    |E    F♯m          |
                  We'll sing and dance to Mother Nature's    songs.
                A                    B                    ‖
                  I don't want this feeling to go away.


Interlude       E                    |                |F♯m              |                    |

                E                    |                |F♯m              |                    ‖


                E                |
Verse 2         Who's to say      I can't do everything?
                      |F♯m          |                            |E              |
                Well, I can try      and as I roll along I be - gin to find
                E                        |F♯m            |
                  Things aren't always just what they seem.




                                      ‖E      F♯m              |
Chorus 2        I want to turn the whole thing upside    down.
                A           B                |E     F♯m            |
                  I'll find the things they say just can't be    found.
                A           B                |E    F♯m            |
                  I'll share this love I find with every - one.
                A           B                    |E    F♯m          |
                  We'll sing and dance to Mother Nature's    songs.
```

Bridge

```
           A                     B                ‖G♯m
             This world keeps spinning and there's no
                        |F♯m
           Time to waste.
                        |G♯m
           Well, it all
             |A                      B                    ‖
           Keeps spinning, spinning, 'round and 'round and
```

Chorus 3

```
           E     F♯m          |
           Upside    down.
           A                   B              |E     F♯m         |
             Who's to say what's impossible and can't be    found?
           A                B                |E       |        |F♯m       |
             I don't want this feeling to go away.
           F♯m                       |E      |        |F♯m
                 Please don't go away.
             |F♯m              A       |E         ‖
           Is this how it's sup - posed to be?
```

Wasting Time

Words and Music by
Jack Johnson, Merlo Podlewski and Adam Topol

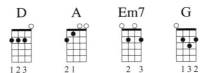

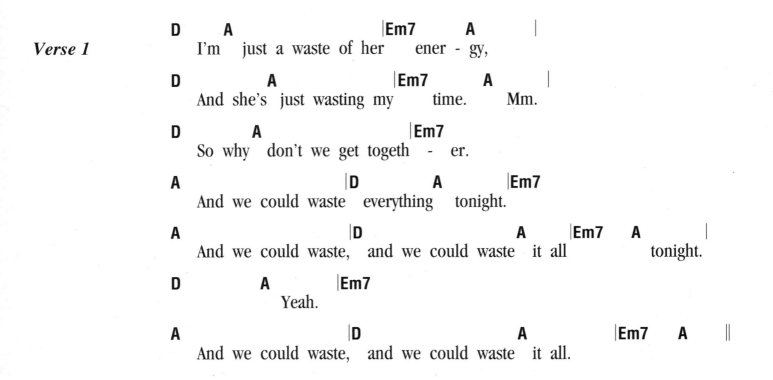

Verse 1

D   A |Em7   A |
I'm   just a waste of her   ener - gy,

D   A |Em7   A |
And she's just wasting my   time.   Mm.

D   A |Em7
So why don't we get togeth - er.

A |D   A |Em7
And we could waste everything   tonight.

A |D   A |Em7 A |
And we could waste, and we could waste it all   tonight.

D   A |Em7
              Yeah.

A |D   A |Em7 A ||
And we could waste, and we could waste it all.

```
                D           A                    |Em7       A          |
Verse 2         I don't   pretend to know what you know.    No, no.

                D               A                  |Em7                    A          |
                Now, please   don't pretend to know      what's on my mind.

                D               A                 |Em7                      A
                If we al - ready knew everything      that everybody knows,

                          |D           A              |Em7     A
                We would have   nothing to learn    tonight.

                           |D           A              |Em7      A
                And we would have    nothing to show tonight.


                      ‖G
Chorus          Oh, but ev - 'rybody thinks

                                    |A
                That everybody knows about ev - 'rybody else.

                                   |G
                (But) nobody knows an - ything about themselves,

                     |A                                      |
                'Cause they're   all worried about everybody else, yeah.

                D        A        |Em7      A          |
                     Yeah.              Mm.

                D        A        |Em7      A         ‖
                         Oh.
```

Verse 3

```
       D         A              |Em7      A          |
       Love's  just a waste of our    ener - gy, yeah,

       D              A              |Em7       A          |
       And this life's  just a waste of our      time.

       D        A           |Em7
       So why   don't we get togeth - er?

       A                    |D        A        |Em7
       And we could waste   everything   tonight.

       A                    |D              A        |Em7
       And we could waste,   and we could waste   it all.
```

Chorus

```
       A              ‖G
       Yeah, but ev - 'rybody thinks

                              |A
       That everybody knows about ev - 'rybody else.

                              |G
       No, no, nobody knows an - ything about themselves,

                  |A                                    |
       'Cause they're   all worried about everybody else, yeah.

       D    A  |Em7  A     |
            Oh.

       D    A                  |Em7    A      ‖
            And we could waste…
```

Outro

```
       D                      A           |
       Do, do, do, do, do, do, do.

       Em7                    A              |
       Do, do,. do, do, do, do, do, do, do, do, do.

       D                      A           |
       Do, do, do, do, do, do, do.

       Em7                    A                |D              ‖
       Do, do, do, do, do, do, do, do, do, do, do, do, do.
```

116

You and Your Heart

Words and Music by
Jack Johnson

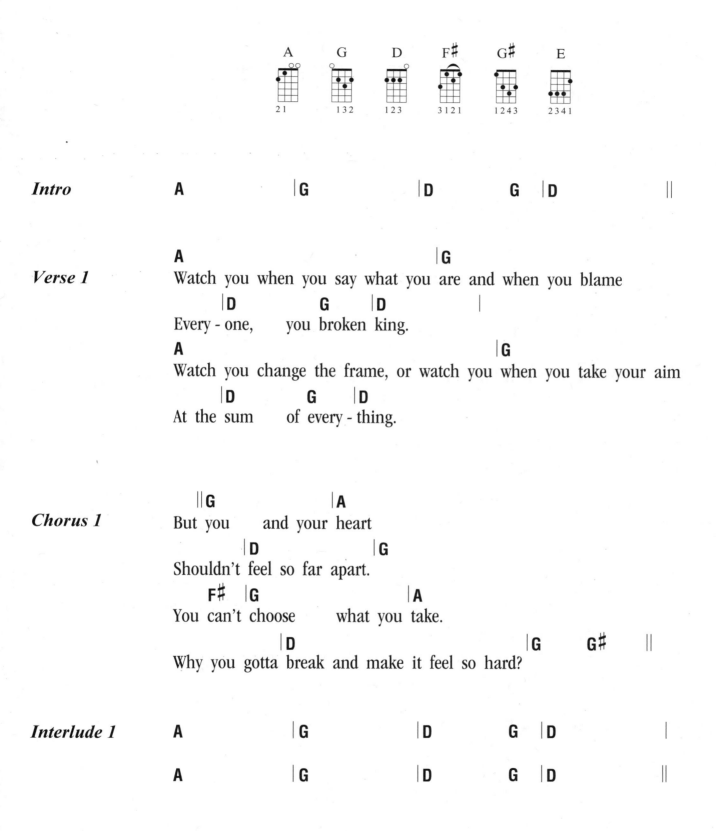

Intro   A |G |D   G |D ||

Verse 1

    A |G
Watch you when you say what you are and when you blame
     |D   G |D |
Every - one,   you broken king.
   A |G
Watch you change the frame, or watch you when you take your aim
     |D   G |D
At the sum   of every - thing.

Chorus 1

      ||G |A
But you   and your heart
     |D |G
Shouldn't feel so far apart.
   F# |G |A
You can't choose   what you take.
       |D |G   G# ||
Why you gotta break and make it feel so hard?

Interlude 1   A |G |D   G |D |

                  A |G |D   G |D ||

Verse 2

  A   **|G**
Lay there in the street like broken glass reflecting pieces
    |D   **G** **|D**
Of the sun; you're not the flame.
      |A   **|G**
You cut the people passing by because you know what you don't like.
     |D   **G** **|D**
It's just so easy. It's just so easy.

Chorus 2

    ||G   **|A**
But you and your heart
      |D   **|G**
Shouldn't feel so far apart.
   F♯ **|G**   **|A**
You can't choose what you take.
      |D   **|G**
Why you gotta break and make it feel so hard?

Chorus 3

   F♯ **||G**   **|A**
Oh, and you and your heart
      |D   **|G**
Shouldn't feel so far apart.
   F♯ **|G**   **|A**
You can't choose what you take.
      |D   **|G** **G♯** **||**
Why you gotta break and make it feel so hard?

Interlude 2   **A** **D**   **|A** **D**   **|A** **D**   **|A** **D**   **|**

          E   **|**

Outro

```
           ‖A              D
You draw so many lines in   the sand,
        |A             D
Lost the fingernails on   your hands.
           |A              D
How you gonna scratch an - y backs?
      |A               D              |E
Better hope the tide will   take our lines a - way.
        |E                  |
Take all    our lines and…
A        D       |A       D              |
Hope the   tide will take our   lines a-…
A        D       |A       D       |E
Hope the   tide will take our   lines a - way.
        |E              |A         ‖
Take all    our lines away.
```

THE HOTTEST TAB SONGBOOKS AVAILABLE FOR GUITAR & BASS!

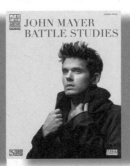

from

cherry lane
music company

Guitar Transcriptions

02501410	The Black Keys – Attack & Release	$19.99
02501500	The Black Keys – A Collection	$19.99
02500702	Best of Black Label Society	$22.95
02500842	Black Label Society – Mafia	$19.95
02500116	Black Sabbath – Riff by Riff	$14.95
02500882	Blues Masters by the Bar	$19.95
02500921	Best of Joe Bonamassa	$22.95
02501510	Joe Bonamassa Collection	$24.99
02501272	Bush – 16 Stone	$21.95
02500179	Mary Chapin Carpenter Authentic Guitar Style of	$16.95
02500336	Eric Clapton – Just the Riffs	$12.99
02501565	Coheed and Cambria – Year of the Black Rainbow	$19.99
02501439	David Cook	$22.99
02500684	Dashboard Confessional – A Mark • A Mission • A Brand • A Scar	$19.95
02500689	Dashboard Confessional – The Places You Have Come to Fear the Most	$17.95
02500843	Dashboard Confessional – The Swiss Army Romance	$17.95
02501481	Brett Dennen – So Much More	$19.99
02506878	John Denver Anthology for Easy Guitar Revised Edition	$15.95
02506901	John Denver Authentic Guitar Style	$14.95
02500984	John Denver – Folk Singer	$19.95
02506928	John Denver – Greatest Hits for Fingerstyle Guitar	$14.95
02500632	John Denver Collection Strum & Sing Series	$9.95
02501448	Best of Ronnie James Dio	$22.99
02500607	The Best of Dispatch	$19.95
02500198	Best of Foreigner	$19.95
02500990	Donavon Frankenreiter	$19.95
02501242	Guns N' Roses – Anthology	$24.95
02506953	Guns N' Roses – Appetite for Destruction	$22.95
02501286	Guns N' Roses Complete, Volume 1	$24.95
02501287	Guns N' Roses Complete, Volume 2	$24.95
02506211	Guns N' Roses – 5 of the Best, Vol. 1	$12.95
02506975	Guns N' Roses – GN'R Lies	$19.95
02500299	Guns N' Roses – Live Era '87-'93 Highlights	$24.95
02501193	Guns N' Roses – Use Your Illusion I	$24.99
02501194	Guns N' Roses – Use Your Illusion II	$24.95
02506325	Metallica – The Art of Kirk Hammett	$17.95
02500939	Hawthorne Heights – The Silence in Black and White	$19.95
02500458	Best of Warren Haynes	$22.95
02500476	Warren Haynes – Guide to Slide Guitar	$17.95

02500387	Best of Heart	$19.95
02500016	The Art of James Hetfield	$17.95
02500873	Jazz for the Blues Guitarist	$14.95
02500554	Jack Johnson – Brushfire Fairytales	$19.95
02500831	Jack Johnson – In Between Dreams	$19.95
02500653	Jack Johnson – On and On	$19.95
02501139	Jack Johnson – Sleep Through the Static	$19.95
02500858	Jack Johnson – Strum & Sing	$14.99
02501564	Jack Johnson – To the Sea	$19.99
02500380	Lenny Kravitz – Greatest Hits	$19.95
02500024	Best of Lenny Kravitz	$19.95
02500129	Adrian Legg – Pickin' 'n' Squintin'	$19.95
02500362	Best of Little Feat	$19.95
02501094	Hooks That Kill – The Best of Mick Mars & Mötley Crüe	$19.95
02500305	Best of The Marshall Tucker Band	$19.95
02501077	Dave Matthews Band – Anthology	$24.99
02501357	Dave Matthews Band – Before These Crowded Streets	$19.95
02501279	Dave Matthews Band – Crash	$19.95
02501266	Dave Matthews Band – Under the Table and Dreaming	$19.95
02500131	Dave Matthews/Tim Reynolds – Live at Luther College, Vol. 1	$19.95
02500611	Dave Matthews/Tim Reynolds – Live at Luther College, Vol. 2	$22.95
02501502	John Mayer – Battle Studies	$22.99
02500986	John Mayer – Continuum	$22.99
02500705	John Mayer – Heavier Things	$22.95
02500705	John Mayer – Heavier Things	$22.95
02500529	John Mayer – Room for Squares	$22.95
02506965	Metallica – ...And Justice for All	$22.99
02501267	Metallica – Death Magnetic	$24.95
02506210	Metallica – 5 of the Best/Vol.1	$12.95
02506235	Metallica – 5 of the Best/Vol. 2	$12.95
02500070	Metallica – Garage, Inc.	$24.95
02507018	Metallica – Kill 'Em All	$19.99
02501232	Metallica – Live: Binge & Purge	$19.95
02501275	Metallica – Load	$24.95
02507920	Metallica – Master of Puppets	$19.95
02501195	Metallica – Metallica	$22.95
02501297	Metallica – ReLoad	$24.95
02507019	Metallica – Ride the Lightning	$19.95
02500279	Metallica – S&M Highlights	$24.95
02500638	Metallica – St. Anger	$24.95
02500577	Molly Hatchet – 5 of the Best	$9.95
02501529	Monte Montgomery Collection	$24.99
02500846	Best of Steve Morse Band and Dixie Dregs	$19.95

02500765	Jason Mraz – Waiting for My Rocket to Come	$19.95
02501324	Jason Mraz – We Sing, We Dance, We Steal Things.	$22.99
02500448	Best of Ted Nugent	$19.95
02500707	Ted Nugent – Legendary Licks	$19.95
02500844	Best of O.A.R. (Of a Revolution)	$22.95
02500348	Ozzy Osbourne – Blizzard of Ozz	$19.95
02501277	Ozzy Osbourne – Diary of a Madman	$19.95
02507904	Ozzy Osbourne/Randy Rhoads Tribute	$22.95
02500524	The Bands of Ozzfest	$16.95
02500680	Don't Stop Believin': The Steve Perry Anthology	$22.95
02500025	Primus Anthology – A-N (Guitar/Bass)	$19.95
02500091	Primus Anthology – O-Z (Guitar/Bass)	$19.95
02500468	Primus – Sailing the Seas of Cheese	$19.95
02500875	Queens of the Stone Age – Lullabies to Paralyze	$24.95
02500608	Queens of the Stone Age – Songs for the Deaf	$19.95
02500659	The Best of Bonnie Raitt	$24.95
02501268	Joe Satriani	$22.95
02501299	Joe Satriani – Crystal Planet	$24.95
02500306	Joe Satriani – Engines of Creation	$22.95
02501205	Joe Satriani – The Extremist	$22.95
02507029	Joe Satriani – Flying in a Blue Dream	$22.95
02501155	Joe Satriani – Professor Satchafunkilus and the Musterion of Rock	$24.95
02500544	Joe Satriani – Strange Beautiful Music	$22.95
02500920	Joe Satriani – Super Colossal	$22.95
02506959	Joe Satriani – Surfing with the Alien	$19.95
02500560	Joe Satriani Anthology	$24.95
02501255	Best of Joe Satriani	$19.95
02501238	Sepultura – Chaos A.D.	$19.95
02500188	Best of the Brian Setzer Orchestra	$19.95
02500985	Sex Pistols – Never Mind the Bollocks, Here's the Sex Pistols	$19.95
02501230	Soundgarden – Superunknown	$19.95
02500956	The Strokes – Is This It	$19.95
02501586	The Sword – Age of Winters	$19.99
02500799	Tenacious D	$19.95
02501035	Tenacious D – The Pick of Destiny	$19.95
02501263	Tesla – Time's Making Changes	$19.95
02501147	30 Easy Spanish Guitar Solos	$14.99
02500561	Learn Funk Guitar with Tower of Power's Jeff Tamelier	$19.95
02501440	Derek Trucks – Already Free	$24.99
02501007	Keith Urban – Love, Pain & The Whole Crazy Thing	$24.95
02500636	The White Stripes – Elephant	$19.95
02501095	The White Stripes – Icky Thump	$19.95
02500583	The White Stripes – White Blood Cells	$19.95
02501092	Wilco – Sky Blue Sky	$22.95
02500431	Best of Johnny Winter	$19.95
02500949	Wolfmother	$22.95
02500199	Best of Zakk Wylde	$22.99
02500700	Zakk Wylde – Legendary Licks	$19.95

Bass Transcriptions

02501108	Bass Virtuosos	$19.95
02500117	Black Sabbath – Riff by Riff Bass	$17.95
02506966	Guns N' Roses – Appetite for Destruction	$19.95
02501522	John Mayer Anthology for Bass, Vol. 1	$24.99
02500639	Metallica – St. Anger	$19.95
02500771	Best of Rancid for Bass	$17.95
02501120	Best of Tower of Power for Bass	$19.95
02500317	Victor Wooten Songbook	$22.95

Transcribed Scores

02500424	The Best of Metallica	$24.95
02500883	Mr. Big – Lean into It	$24.95

See your local music dealer or contact:

cherry lane music company

EXCLUSIVELY DISTRIBUTED BY
HAL•LEONARD CORPORATION
7777 W. BLUEMOUND RD. P.O. BOX 13819 MILWAUKEE, WI 53213

Prices, contents, and availability subject to change without notice.

0211